TWENTIETH CENTURY INTERPRETATIONS
OF

P A M E L A

A Collection of Critical Essays

Edited by

ROSEMARY COWLER

Prentice-Hall, Inc. *Englewood Cliffs, N. J.*

A SPECTRUM BOOK

Contents

Introduction

by Rosemary Cowler

I

As recently as 1956, Professor Alan D. McKillop, the dean of
Richardson scholars, was writing, "The history of Richardson's reputation . . . shows . . . that the generation of Jane Austen and Lady
Louisa Stuart, Coleridge and Hazlitt and Lamb, read him with greater
intelligence and discrimination than it has been his fortune to meet
with since, unless indeed the balance is being redressed at the present
time." [1] This volume of essays is a vindication of that "indeed"—a
testimony to the significant contemporary reassessment of Richardson
and of Richardson's most troublesome novel. In large part, this modern critical interest is a reflection of a broader activity, the whole
post-World War II effort of re-editing, re-interpreting, and re-evaluat-
ing the literature of the eighteenth century. But even here the study
of the early novel has been long overdue, so that Richardson is sharing with Defoe and especially with Fielding a very current renais-
sance. How immediate can be judged by the chronology of the selections that follow, where only two of the contributions antedate Mr.
McKillop's comment. One has very much the sense of reading "to the
moment."

Happily, Richardson's "sharing" with Fielding is in this instance
a figure of speech, not the yoking that has for so long complicated
the literary histories of the two men. When, just two centuries ago,
Dr. Johnson made one of his more famous Richardson-Fielding pronouncements—" 'that there was as great a difference between them
as between a man who knew how a watch was made, and a man who
could tell the hour by looking on the dial-plate' " [2]—instead of setting
them apart, he helped link them inexorably together. The comparison, from the outset inimical, persisted, and became a means of
examining and extolling one author at the expense of the other: Richardson the moralist and sentimentalist against Fielding the realist

---

[1] Alan Dugald McKillop, *The Early Masters of English Fiction* (Lawrence, Kansas,
1956), p. 97.
[2] *Boswell's Life of Johnson*, ed. G. B. Hill (Oxford, 1887), II, 49.

and stylist, with Fielding, despite Dr. Johnson's authoritative pref-
erence, carrying the field and dragging Richardson behind him..

Today Fielding's renewed popularity might suggest the complete
submergence of Richardson except that modern critics have rejected
the facile, conventional definitions. For example, Sheldon Sacks under-
takes in this volume a refutation of easy assumptions about the relation of the novelist's art to his ethical convictions, and William Park
is represented by a section from "Fielding *and* Richardson," an article
which plots the common ground between them. Ironically, even some
of the critics who do retain or on occasion utilize the old joint perspective have reversed the familiar polarity. No longer is it Fielding
the realist and Richardson the mere moralist; judgment has come
around full-circle to Dr. Johnson and his distinction between characters of nature and characters only of manners. Such commentators
as Ian Watt,[3] Frank Kermode,[4] and Leslie Fiedler[5] echo him in tracing
true fictional reality back to Richardson, back "into the recesses of
the human heart." [6] Equally important in the development of
Richardson criticism is the critical direction taken by the essays of
this collection. Generally eschewing comparisons—which still are too
often invidious with either-or evaluations and arbitrary judgments—
they turn instead directly to the author and his writings. The concern here is to know Richardson through Richardson: to understand
and appreciate his art by studying him, his world, and his work. In
spite of the inevitable shadow of *Shamela*, Fielding's bawdy parody
of *Pamela*, it is the latter that must come to light—*Pamela*, Richardson's first attempt at fiction and perhaps the first true novel in English
literature.

II

Samuel Richardson was a successful fifty-year-old master printer
when, in 1739, he undertook the work which "changed the course of
English fiction." [7] Two months later, on January 10, 1740, he had
finished *Pamela*, Part I, which he published some ten months after
that. Although the publication was to bring him great fame and lead
him to a sequel and then to two more novels, *Clarissa* and *Sir Charles
Grandison* (the first of which would eventually sustain his reputa-

[3] In *The Rise of the Novel* (Berkeley, 1962), Chapter x, "Realism and the Later
Tradition: a Note."
[4] In "Richardson and Fielding," *Cambridge Journal*, IV (1950); reprinted in
Essays on the Eighteenth-Century Novel, ed. Robert Donald Spector (Bloomington,
Indiana, 1965).
[5] See *View Points*, p. 100.
[6] *Life of Johnson*, II, 49.
[7] McKillop, *Early Masters*, p. 51.

tion), we know very little about his life before *Pamela*. In a celebrated letter to a Dutch correspondent, the Rev. Johannes Stinstra,[8] Richardson tells us that his father was descended from a Surrey family "of middling Note," and that his skill and integrity as a joiner brought him to the attention of the Earl of Shaftesbury and of the Duke of Monmouth, whose beheading caused him to retire from London to Derbyshire, where the future novelist was born, in 1689. Because of financial reverses in the family, the son did not study for the ministry, as his father had planned, but was apprenticed to a printer. Richardson's career from this point sounds like a model for his friend Hogarth's famous series "The Industrious Apprentice" or for his own earliest effort, *The Apprentice's Vade Mecum*, a manual of instruction in diligent behavior. Though Richardson did not persevere to become Lord Mayor of London, like Hogarth's hero, he did like him work hard, he did marry his master's daughter (one of his two marriages), and he did become Master of the Stationers' Company.

Professor William Sale argues that Richardson's eminence in trade was invaluable for his new literary career in that it provided him with an established position from which to view "the interpenetration of the emergent middle class and the surviving aristocracy." [9] This may be true. But even more relevant was another, if not occupation, at least preoccupation of his entire lifetime: his interest in letter writing and in female letter writers. In the same letter to Stinstra, he confided:

> From my earliest Youth, I had a Love of Letter-writing. I was not Eleven Years old, when I wrote, spontaneously, a Letter to a Widow of near Fifty, who, pretending to a Zeal for Religion, & who was a constant Frequenter of Church Ordinances, was continually fomenting Quarrels & Disturbances, by Backbiting & Scandal, among all her Acquaintance. I collected from ye Scripture Texts that made against her. Assuming the Stile and Address of a Person in Years, I exhorted her; I expostulated with her. But my Handwriting was known: I was challenged with it, & owned ye Boldness; for she complained of it to my Mother with Tears. My Mother chid me for the Freedom taken by such a Boy with a Woman of her Years: But knowing that her Son was not of a pert or forward Nature, but, on ye contrary, shy & bashful, she commended my Principles, tho' she censured the Liberty taken.
>
> As a bashful & not forward Boy, I was an early Favourite with all the young Women of Taste & Reading in the Neighbourhood. Half a

[8] This letter, originally printed in McKillop's *Early Masters of English Fiction*, is to be found in *Selected Letters of Samuel Richardson*, ed. John Carroll (Oxford, 1964), pp. 228—35. For biographical detail and general background, McKillop's book, as well as his earlier work, *Samuel Richardson: Printer and Novelist* (Chapel Hill, 1936), is invaluable.

[9] William M. Sale, *Samuel Richardson: Master Printer* (Ithaca, New York, 1950), p. 1.

Dozen of them when met to Work with their Needles, used, when they
got a Book they liked, & thought I should, to borrow me to read to
them; their Mothers sometimes with them; & both Mothers & Daughters
used to be pleased with the Observations they put me upon making.

I was not more than Thirteen when three of these young Women,
unknown to each other, having an high Opinion of my Taciturnity, revealed to me their Love Secrets, in order to induce me to give them
Copies to write after, or correct, for Answers to their Lovers Letters:
Nor did any of them ever know, that I was the Secretary to the others.
I have been directed to chide, & even repulse, when an Offence was
either taken or given, at the very time that the Heart of the Chider or
Repulser was open before me, overflowing with Esteem & Affection; &
the fair Repulser dreading to be taken at her Word; directing *this* Word,
or *that* Expression, to be softened or changed.[10]

Under these circumstances it was altogether appropriate that this
printer and occasional writer should be urged by two bookseller
friends to compose a volume of model letters for the benefit of the
untutored. What were to be merely sample letters, however, turned
into something more. "Will it be any Harm said I"—this is Richardson
explaining what happened—"in a Piece you want to be written so low,
if we should instruct them how they should think & act in common
Cases, as well as indite? They were the more urgent with me to
begin the little Volume, for this Hint. I set about it, & in the Progress
of it, writing two or three Letters to instruct handsome Girls, who were
obliged to go out to Service, as we phrase it, how to avoid the Snares
that might be laid against their Virtue; the above story [i.e., of
Pamela[11]] recurred to my Thought: And hence sprung Pamela." [12]

As a springboard, these events proved both fortunate and unfortunate. That the novel grew out of Richardson's deepest consciousness—
his great involvement in the feminine mind and world—and that it
took expression in the form most natural to him, the letter, is the
reason that it is so accomplished a book for a first endeavor. For all
its weaknesses, there is a sense of professional expertise. On the other
hand, Richardson was limited by the established pattern of a recalled
story; when he was free to manipulate his plot, as in *Clarissa*—totally
his own imaginative creation—he was more successful in his narrative.

[10] *Selected Letters of Samuel Richardson*, ed. John Carroll (Oxford, 1964), pp.
230–1. Reprinted by permission of the Clarendon Press, Oxford.

[11] "The Story of Pamela had some slight Foundation in Truth. Several Persons of
Rank were guessed at, as having in my Mind sat for the two Principal Characters
in that Piece: But no one Conjecture came near the Truth; nor was it likely that it
should; for I myself knew no more of the Story, than what I recollected a Gentleman
told me of it Fifteen Years before I sat down to write it; & as it was related to him
by an Innkeeper in the neighbourhood of the happy Pair; & which Gentleman had
been, at the Time, several Years dead." (*Selected Letters*, p. 232; a longer account
of this story is given in another letter, pp. 39–40.)

[12] *Ibid.*, p. 232.

More serious still was the difficulty of translating into fiction material that originated for a more edifying purpose. As Richardson noted in another letter (letters played as essential a part in his life as in his fictions): "In my Scheme I have generally taken Human Nature *as it is . . .*"[13]—a far different matter from a manual to outline life as it should be. So while the title page of the novel announces its conduct-book intentions, *Pamela* is no more a treatise than Pamela is the archetype of every handsome serving maid. Or so it is in Part I; in Part II—the saga of Pamela's married life—Richardson does turn to a conduct-book perspective (perhaps as a vindication of Part I against attacks like *Shamela*)[14] and the novel suffers accordingly, with readers left confused by the shift in tone and technique.

In yet another letter—for Richardson did like to expound on his writing and, also, to solicit advice not usually heeded—he commented further:

> Little did I think, at first, of making one, much less two volumes of it. But, when I began to recollect what had, so many years before, been told me by my friend, I thought the story, if written in an easy and natural manner, suitably to the simplicity of it, might possibly introduce a new species of writing, that might possibly turn young people into a course of reading different from the pomp and parade of romance writing, and dismissing the improbable and marvellous, with which novels generally abound, might tend to promote the cause of religion and virtue. I therefore gave way to enlargement: and so Pamela became as you see her.[15]

With this turn from the "improbable and marvellous," Richardson did produce "a new species of writing," and with this realism the modern novel comes into being. As Ian Watt in his *Rise of the Novel* points out, the primary convention of the novel form in general is that it must give "a full and authentic report of human experience, and is therefore under an obligation to satisfy its reader with such details of the story as the individuality of the actors concerned, the particulars of the times and places of their actions, details which are presented through a more largely referential use of language than is common in other literary forms."[16] There are elements in *Pamela*— the heroine's romantic name and the limited specificity of time,[17] to name only two—which suggest that in this work realism is not completely achieved, perhaps deliberately not achieved. Yet in taking a heroine from the real world and exposing her to possible and plausible

---

[13] *Ibid.*, p. 47.
[14] See Owen Jenkins' argument in *View Points*, pp. 105–8.
[15] *Selected Letters*, p. 41.
[16] Watt, *Rise of the Novel*, p. 32.
[17] See Ian Watt's "Naming of Characters" and John Samuel Bullen's "Time in *Pamela*" in *View Points*, pp. 98–100, 108–10.

adventures lively enough to "catch young and airy Minds, and when Passions run high in them, to shew how they may be directed to laudable Meanings and Purposes," [18] Richardson did hit upon something new, the perfect combination for his age and its gradually expanding reading public. To have pleasure *and* edification was a novel treat; it was to have one's cake and eat it too.

An eager audience made quite a feast of it. So popular was *Pamela* that it was paid the ultimate compliment of numerous adaptations, imitations, dramatizations, translations, burlesques, parodies, travesties—all that vast bulk of outpourings that comprise the Pamelist-Anti-Pamelist activities,[19] the most distinguished examples of which are Fielding's *Shamela* and *Joseph Andrews*. It was when outsiders were even planning a sequel to the story that Richardson was driven to protect himself and his heroine with his own continuation, the original Volumes III and IV, published in December of 1741. The combination of realism and morality that sold so well in England won Richardson a continental reputation too. During a period in France characterized by a vogue for English fiction, the success of Richardson's first novel is still remarkable. A study of several hundred catalogues from eighteenth-century French private libraries has shown that *Pamela* outranks all other English items, with mention 78 times in comparison to 77 entries for *Tom Jones*, 69 for *Clarissa*, 44 for *Grandison*, and 40 for *Joseph Andrews*.[20] Indeed the works of Richardson and Fielding were to do much to provide respectability for the novel as a genre in France, although the English models were often criticized for their social vulgarity and brutality.[21]

An account of *Pamela's* fortunes across the seas is equally interesting —and, in this review of the novel's past, nicely appropriate for an American volume devoted to its present and future. What more fitting than that *Pamela* should be the first novel printed in America, and by Benjamin Franklin? "Though *Tom Jones* had to wait fifty-four years for an American edition, *Pamela* was published in Philadelphia only four years after its appearance in England." [22] And what more fitting again than to realize that American fiction took its beginnings from the Richardsonian mode? If, for better or worse (much worse, according to Leslie Fiedler[23]), the American novel later took a different

[18] *Selected Letters*, p. 46.
[19] For an account of the writings that grew out of the success of *Pamela*, see Bernard Kreissman, *Pamela-Shamela* (University of Nebraska Press, 1960).
[20] Georges May, "The Influence of English Fiction on the French Mid-Eighteenth-Century Novel," *Aspects of the Eighteenth Century*, ed. Earl R. Wasserman (Baltimore, Maryland, 1965), p. 270.
[21] *Ibid.*, pp. 274–80.
[22] Leslie A. Fiedler, *Love and Death in the American Novel* (New York, 1960), p. 44.
[23] See *Love and Death in the American Novel*.

direction, at least now in the twentieth century, we are having a critical reunion.

III

The new critical perspectives that are so essential for Richardson studies in general are nowhere more desperately needed than for *Pamela,* which has always proved a "provoking" problem novel. While everyone agrees that *Clarissa* is Richardson's masterpiece, a classic in its own right, and while no one denies that there are fundamental flaws in the earlier book, with this all consensus and simplicity end. Response to *Pamela* is varied, contradictory, passionate. From the beginning there have been few neutrals in the warfare that developed hard on the publication of the first volumes, when "Pamelist" and "Anti-Pamelist" became part of the language. The furor of *Pamela's* success was matched by the vehemence of the detractions, and there has been remarkably little mellowing over the years. ". . . *Pamela* remains only as a record of a particularly loathsome aspect of bourgeois puritan morality," [24] reads a summary evaluation in a current introduction to the English novel, and so distinguished a critic as Joseph Wood Krutch is reduced to enraged diatribe in his consideration of Pamela and her predicaments.[25] The situation is of course different with her admirers. The wishful and worshipful housemaids who glorified in "their" heroine and the fashionable ladies who fluttered their souvenir "Pamela" fans (entrepreneurs were active even then) have been replaced today by a rather select group of sympathizers who respond with enthusiasm to what is admirable in the novel, but who are also aware of crudities, limitations, and problems. Though even here there is little unanimity of opinion, as the essays that follow clearly reveal.

The controversy about *Pamela* derives from its very fabric and one need not go beyond the title page to be alerted to it. *Pamela: or, Virtue Rewarded,* it begins; and it continues with a typically substantial eighteenth-century sub-title:

> *In a Series of Familiar Letters from a Beautiful Young Damsel, to her Parents. Now first Published in order to cultivate the Principles of Virtue and Religion in the Minds of the Youth of Both Sexes. A Narrative which has its Foundation in Truth and Nature; and at the same time that it agreeably entertains, by a Variety of curious and affecting Incidents, is entirely divested of all those Images, which, in too many*

[24] Arnold Kettle, *An Introduction to the English Novel,* Harper *Torchbooks* (New York, 1960), I, 64–5.

[25] Joseph Wood Krutch, *Five Masters: A Study in the Mutations of the Novel* (Bloomington, Indiana, 1961), pp. 127–32.

Pieces circulated for Amusement only, tend to inflame *the Minds they should* instruct.

"To cultivate the Principles of Virtue and Religion" is one thing; to tie virtue to reward, as the main title pointedly does, is very much another. The suggestive linkage, however negatively posed, between the instructing and inflaming potentialities of those "*curious* and *affecting* Incidents" also hints a disquieting moral ambiguity or coarseness, perhaps a Defoe-like technique of titillating under the guise of edifying.

Certainly the story that follows is on the one hand too simple and on the other not simple enough to be introduced by that title. As the history of a serving maid who, after the death of her patroness-mistress, withstands the blandishments and coercions of the rakish young aristocratic heir and, by steadfastly preserving her virginity, foils his seduction schemes and gains him in marriage, to live happily and somewhat self-righteously ever after, it might do for a fairy tale;[26] but as a representation of serious moral themes, it all too plainly invites the charge of moral faking that Fielding made with his *Shamela—An Apology for the Life of Mrs. Shamela Andrews: In which, the many notorious Falsehoods and Misrepresentations of a Book called* Pamela, *are exposed and refuted; and all the matchless Arts of that young Politician set in a true and just Light.* In his phrase "that young Politician" Fielding indicates how far for him Pamela's so-called "Principles of Virtue and Religion" have indeed become means and not ends, her true ends being status and power.

And yet, a parody like *Shamela* revealed its own crudity in its interpretation of the personality of Richardson's heroine. For this, despite the plot, is perceptively and subtly drawn. Pamela's morality may be limited to a rather shallow prudence and her insight may be naive, the product of a narrow ethic, but to attribute this to conscious hypocrisy and present her as a designing slut, as Fielding did, was to distort the original grotesquely if, for the moment, amusingly. What makes Shamela invalid, it can be argued, is that Pamela, though hardly exemplary as a guide to the good life, is a real—and because real often contradictory—person. She is a very young, sensitive girl, experiencing for the first time and under extraordinarily trying circumstances some of the moral complexities and inconsistencies that make up actual adult life.[27] In the face of her own emotional awakening, with all the attendant confused, unfathomable impulses; in the distressing ambiguity of her social position, having been indulged and educated

[26] The fairy-tale quality of parts of the novel has been pointed out by Frank Bradbrook, "Samuel Richardson," *From Dryden to Johnson,* ed. Boris Ford, The Pelican Guide to English Literature, IV, 295.

[27] Ian Watt takes a similar stand in a B.B.C. talk, "Samuel Richardson," published

beyond her station by her dead mistress, who "bequeathed" her to the care of her new "protector"; in her complete isolation, cut off from parents who are, in any case, in no position to intercede or to provide a future for her at home, nothing is more natural than that in times of confusion and peril she should honestly revert to her early training and take refuge in a stubbornly materialistic morality. Literal-minded though she may be about her virtue, it does represent the one absolute to which she can cling. It is her talisman—to coin a figure that is at least more fortunate than the "jewel" to which her parents allude.

The jewel reference, with all its dubious commercial implications, is a prime example of the way Richardson renders himself vulnerable to attack. The "Pamelists" who fill these pages defend the book, but they are the first to admit the presence in it of weaknesses and blemishes which cannot be dismissed, though they can be better understood than they have been. The discrepancy (for which we can be thankful) between the promise of the title page and the actuality of the text; the pragmatic tinge to the heroine's "virtue"; the limitations of Mr. B as a character, whether as rake or uxorious husband; the shift in the characterization of Pamela from the vital, witty girl of Part I to the almost allegorical figure of Part II; the difficulties of an epistolary style in which there is only one correspondent, who therefore must constantly advertise her own virtues—these are a few of the defects that no amount of explanation can altogether explain away.

Still, there are substantial compensations. The novel's astounding eighteenth-century popularity is more than just an interesting fact of its history. We can today share with those servant-girl readers the drama of the early episodes, even if we must at the same time confess, as Dr. Johnson did—in a famous rejoinder to a complaint, no doubt heartfelt, that Richardson can be tedious—" 'Why, Sir, if you were to read Richardson for the story, your impatience would be so much fretted that you would hang yourself. But you must read him for the sentiment and consider the story as only giving occasion to the

---

in *The Listener*, LXXIII (1965) and later reprinted in a collection *The Novelist as Innovator* (B.B.C., 1965):

So one way out of the dilemma which Fielding's *Shamela* seems to pose is to accept the view that Pamela is neither all superego, as Richardson sometimes suggests, nor all libido, which would be one way of putting Fielding's views. Instead, she is merely, like everyone else, a mixture. And so, before we assume that her contradictory attitudes must be evidence of hypocrisy, one must be very sure that they are not merely the usual human muddle—a muddle in the person, not the book, I should add. For Pamela's motivations and actions throughout seem to me to be wholly credible and consistent with any adequately complex notion of human behaviour. And we have considerable evidence that Richardson himself was fully conscious of the ambiguities of the human mind. (Pp. 178-9.)

sentiment.' " [28] What Johnson here calls sentiment we would nowadays call the insightful, detailed revelation of character and feeling which carries a reader to the core of the heroine's troubled inner world. Ian Watt, in a discussion of the complexity and authenticity of her characterization, sees her in the tradition of Emma Woodhouse, David Copperfield, Stephen Dedalus and Paul Morel—"young protagonists gradually learning to relate dissonant impulses to each other, to circumstance, and to the people they meet." [29] Pamela is in good company in this statement and she deserves to be there.

Mr. Watt also calls attention to the quiet artistry of the work. It has become almost dogma that *Clarissa* is a controlled artistic effort but that *Pamela,* written some seven years before, is not, and that whatever excellences it possesses are largely the product of chance or of genius asserting itself in spite of the author, who really did not know what he was about. The studies in this volume should do much to disprove this assumption, but particularly effective as a challenge to it is Mr. Watt's analysis of the opening paragraph of the novel. [30] In what might seem merely a random, artless recounting of events is, he demonstrates, a very art*ful* narrative skill:

> The real case for Richardson must be made . . . on the grounds, I suggest, that behind the aimless prattle there is also a mind in control—and in control, not only of a convincing narrative voice, but of the shape of the fiction as a whole. A second look at the passage reveals, for example, that all the themes of the story are sounded, and sounded in a way that expresses the nature of their eventual conflict. There is the economic motive, Pamela's dependence, and her fear of being forced to return and be a clog on her parents. There is the class issue: Pamela's awed respect for her social betters and her feeling of being

[28] *Life of Johnson,* II, 175.
[29] Watt, "Samuel Richardson," p. 179.
[30] Dear Father and Mother,
    I have great trouble, and some comfort to acquaint you with. The trouble is that my good lady died of the illness I mentioned to you, and left us all much grieved for the loss of her: she was a dear good lady, and kind to all us her servants. Much I feared, that as I was taken by her ladyship to wait upon her person, I should be quite destitute again, and forced to return to you and my poor mother, who have enough to do to maintain yourselves; and, as my lady's goodness had put me to write and cast accounts, and made me a little expert at my needle, and otherwise qualified above my degree, it was not every family that could have found a place that your poor Pamela was fit for: but God, whose graciousness to us we have so often experienced, put it into my good lady's heart, just an hour before she expired, to recommend to my young master all her servants, one by one; and when it came to my turn to be recommended (for I was sobbing and crying at her pillow), she could only say—"My dear son!" and so broke off a little; and then recovering, "remember my poor Pamela."—And these were some of her last words. O how my eyes run! Don't wonder to see the paper so blotted. (Samuel Richardson, *Pamela,* Everyman Edition [London, 1966], I, 1.)

herself 'qualified above her degree'—she is already on the way up and scrubbing floors is out. Then there is Pamela's obtrusive religious piety, coupled with her complacent assurance that God's graciousness is especially extended to her and her family. And finally there is the ironic climax that what God most specifically does for her is to 'put it into my good lady's heart . . . [to] say "My dear son! . . . remember my poor Pamela.' " [31]

Less subtle than this thematic structuring but, nevertheless, important evidence of Richardson's craftsmanship in *Pamela* is his ability to use language to delineate character. If this heroine can be—and too often is—sententious, she can also be delightfully natural, colloquial, and sprightly, as her wit attests. In her comments to her parents about the behavior of others of her sex in her situation:

> But, dear father and mother, what sort of creatures must the women-kind be, do you think, to give way to such wickedness? Why, this it is that makes every one to be thought of alike: and, a-lack-a-day! what a world we live in! for it is grown more a wonder that the men are *resisted,* than that the women *comply.* This, I suppose, makes me such a Sauce-box, and Bold-face, and a creature; and all because I won't be a Sauce-box and Bold-face indeed.[32]

and equally in her retort to the unctuous apologies of the servant who has betrayed her:

> "Mighty well, Mr. Robert!" said I; "I never saw an execution but once; and then the hangman asked the poor creature's pardon, wiped his mouth as you do, pleaded his duty, and then calmly tucked up the criminal. But I am no criminal, as you know; if I could have thought it my duty to obey a wicked master in his unlawful commands, I had saved you all the merit of this vile service." [33]

we have two examples of her characteristic keenness and salt: this is no Pollyanna. But Richardson's greatest achievement with her is in another tone, in communicating the emotional distress of her plight, where the real dangers are within, not without:

> O my exulting heart! how it throbs in my bosom, as if it would reproach me for so lately unbraiding it for giving way to the love of so dear a gentleman. "But take care thou art not too credulous, neither, O fond believer! Things that we wish are apt to gain a too ready credence with us. This sham marriage is not yet cleared up: the vile Mrs. Jewkes may yet instigate the mind of this master: his pride of heart

---

[31] Watt, "Samuel Richardson," p. 177. It is interesting to note that B.L. Reid also cites this opening letter as a subtle example of "the ordered craft of art" (see pp. 33–41).

[32] *Pamela,* I, 57.

[33] *Ibid.,* I, 92.

and condition may again take place; and a man that could, in so *little* a space, first love me, then hate, then banish me his house, and now send for me again, in such affectionate terms, may *still* waver, may *still* deceive thee. Therefore will I not acquit thee yet O credulous, fluttering, throbbing mischief! that art so ready to believe what thou wishest; I charge thee to keep better guard than thou hast lately done, and lead me not to follow too implicitly thy flattering and desirable impulses." Thus foolishly dialogued I with my heart; and yet, all the time, this heart is Pamela.[34]

Justly famous as Richardson is for such mining of the female heart, he can also produce the coarse sensibility of the vulgar-tongued Mrs. Jewkes, and he approaches Fielding's gusto, too, in one very unexpected character sketch, that of Sir Simon Darnford. Surprisingly, critics rarely mention this engaging rake, trying to hold his own against a household of women and against old age with a toothless vigor that is touching as well as amusing:

> But what must I do?—I'd be glad at any rate to stand in your lady's graces [i.e., those of Pamela, now Mrs. B], that I would; nor would I be the last rake libertine unreformed by her example, which I suppose will make virtue the fashion, if she goes on as she does. But here I have been used to cut a joke and toss the squib about; and, as far as I know, it has helped to keep me alive in the midst of pains and aches, and with two women-grown girls, and the rest of the mortifications that will attend on *advanced years*; for I won't (hang me if I will) give it up as absolute *old age*!
>
> But now, it seems, I must leave all this off, or I must be mortified with a looking glass held before me, and every wrinkle must be made as conspicuous as a furrow —And what, pray, is to succeed to this reformation? —I can neither fast nor pray, I doubt. —And besides, if my stomach and my jest depart from me, farewell, Sir Simon Darnford! [35]

In the blend of comedy-pathos here there is more than just the echo of situation and phrase to recall another unregenerate, old Sir John Falstaff; and one is led to remember that in their art, Richardson and Shakespeare have often been associated.[36]

*   *   *

In short, this mid-eighteenth-century novel can hold a legitimate place even in—especially in—a mid-twentieth-century world—however unlikely that might seem at first. In fact, it is only as *Pamela*'s historical importance (its interest as the "original" novel and as a proving-ground for *Clarissa*) becomes secondary, that its more relevant

[34] *Ibid.*, I, 223.
[35] *Ibid.*, II, 78.
[36] See, for example, Frank Kermode, "Richardson and Fielding."

psychological and artistic significance is being recognized by discerning readers. But because the novel has been as badly abused in reading and study as its heroine in her adventures, the discovery is not an easy one, and this is one instance where critical guidance may be particularly helpful in directing readers to a better understanding and appreciation of a flawed but valuable work. It is on this assumption that the essays which follow have been collected.

PART ONE

Interpretations

Samuel Richardson

by David Daiches

Few writers have suffered as much as Richardson for their historical importance. He is, we all know, "the father of the English novel." Generations of students have noted the fact at university lectures. *Pamela,* they will confide in examinations, is the first true English novel; it is written in epistolary form and tells the story of a virtuous maid who resisted her wealthy master's advances to the point where she won his hand in marriage. *Clarissa* is longer, and tells the story of an equally virtuous lady who was dishonoured by a rake while under the influence of drugs and who consequently died, life after dishonour being impossible. *Sir Charles Grandison,* also long, gives the picture of an ideal gentleman and his ultimate happy marriage with one of the many females who adore him. So much is common knowledge. Most of the students will go on to add that Richardson's morality is bourgeois in the extreme; that Pamela, whose whole endeavour is to sell her chastity in the dearest market, is more of a designing minx than a paragon of virtue, and that Clarissa's languishing into her grave after a purely technical loss of chastity is a typical example of the unacceptable Puritan attitude to sex. Nevertheless, the report will conclude, the fact that all three novels are told in the form of letters passing between the characters enables Richardson to give a fine psychological immediacy to the action; he did understand the female heart, if not the male, and records with commendable subtlety its fluctuations and vagaries; and after all he *is* the father of the English novel. A few more enterprising students might perhaps go on to vindicate Richardson's progenitive claims against those of Defoe or to contrast Richardson's hot-house atmosphere with the fresh air of Fielding. None of them will have read Richardson.

This has been the authorized version of Richardson for some time now, and of course there is some truth in it. Richardson *is* historically important, his morality *is* typical of the middle class of his day, his understanding of the female heart *is* impressive. But the true nature and value of his achievement can be obscured by these parrotted generalizations: it is time we removed the literary historian's ticket from the novels and read them with attention. And it would be as well if in reading them we forgot about "the novel," about the subsequent history of the literary form which Richardson pioneered in England, and concentrated on what was before us. If we did that, we should find, I think, many unexpected patterns of meaning, particularly in *Pamela* and *Clarissa*. We should find that these works were in some ways more closely related to mediaeval saints' lives than to the novel as we now know it, or that they are a kind of *Paradise Lost* and *Paradise Regained,* set not in Eden or the wilderness but in the mundane world of social convention and obligation. Milton and Bunyan were concerned, in their different ways, with the exercise of free-will in resisting temptation and thus achieving salvation, Richardson is concerned with the exercise of prudence in order to achieve success through virtue and thus attain salvation in both worlds. Where the wiles of the devil make this double achievement impossible, as in *Clarissa,* prudence yields to saintliness and the next world provides the only refuge.

The ideas that Richardson employs and manipulates in his novels are: prudence and virtue, gentility and morality, reputation and character. The relation between them is often complex. Gentility is sometimes opposed to morality, sometimes a sign of morality. Reputation is generally the reward of good character but not always a guarantee of it. Prudence and virtue often go together, but sometimes (as in the latter part of *Clarissa*) lead in opposite directions. Richardson is very much aware of the social context; he is, one might say, obsessed with it. Rank mattered to him; the difference between classes was something he could never forget, and his moral patterns are built up against a background of social relationships which provide the most real and ineluctable facts about human life. For Richardson, all the tests of life are public, carried out in full view of society and conditioned by the structure of society. Eden for him is no garden but an estate, and Adam is a landlord with tenants, Eve a lady with social duties and dangers, and the serpent a neighbouring squire who violates the rules of the game by combining the genuine attractiveness of rank with an immoral character. There is no private wrestling with one's soul or with the devil here; Richardson's moral dramas are acted out on a public stage, and any moments of private anguish are promptly communicated by the sufferer to a friend in a letter. The epistolary technique is no incidental device: it is bound up with the social context of Richardson's moral patterns. And if there is no purely private anguish, there is similarly no purely private victory.

Virtue must be recognized to be real, and Clarissa's death is made
into a moral victory and indeed a beatification in virtue of the universal recognition of her saintliness which it produces. Richardson was
the first important English writer to deal with basic moral problems
imaginatively in a detailed social context.

This, then, is what is meant by the claim that Richardson's novels
enshrine an eighteenth-century bourgeois morality. Virtue is consistently related to prudence on the one hand and to reputation on
the other, and the arena of moral struggle is the stratified society of
contemporary England. Further, in the eyes of Richardson and his
fellows the aristocracy is still a class to be envied and aspired to.
Pamela, the serving maid, has her virtue rewarded by marrying into
the squirearchy; Clarissa's upper middle class family want to consoli-
date their position as property owners and achieve a title, and
Clarissa's pursuer, the aristocratic Lovelace, has never any doubt that
marriage to him is a desirable thing for her. Prosperous tradesmen and
master crafsmen may have believed that their class was the sole reposi-
tory of true virtue and respectability in the nation, but the aristocracy
was still admired and looked up to as the class which the successful
bourgeois hoped ultimately to enter. The implications of this double
view of the aristocracy—as representing both rakishness and the
heights of that worldly felicity which was the proper reward of a life
of combined prudence and virtue—can be seen again and again in
the working out of Richardson's plots.

Richardson more than once stated that his primary aim in writing
these novels was moral instruction rather than mere entertainment.
It is perhaps worth quoting his own summary of his intentions, which
he gives us retrospectively in the preface to *Sir Charles Grandison.*
Pamela, he tells us,

> exhibited the beauty and superiority of virtue in an innocent and un-
> polished mind, with the reward which often, even in this life, a protecting
> Providence bestows on goodness. A young woman of low degree, relating
> to her honest parents the severe trials she met with from a master
> who ought to have been the protector, not the assailer of her honour,
> shows the character of a libertine in its truly contemptible light. This
> libertine, however, from the foundation of good principles laid in
> his early years by an excellent mother; by his passion for a virtuous
> young woman; and by her amiable example and unwearied patience,
> when she became his wife, is, after a length of time, perfectly re-
> claimed.

*   *   *

Thus there can be no doubt that Richardson saw his novels as
essentially moral works, comparable, as I have suggested, to mediaeval
saints' lives. But of course a writer's statement of his intentions never

tells us all the important things about a work, particularly when it is
made, as here, after the books have been completed. There was, no
doubt, a certain amount of complacent rationalization about Richardson's descriptions of the nature and purpose of his novels. The
novels themselves are more complex than he ever seems to have realized, works of art by accident, one might almost say, like Bunyan's
Pilgrim's Progress.

*   *   *

Richardson was a printer by trade, and a good and prosperous one.
He was born in 1689, and produced *Pamela*, his first novel, in 1740,
when he was fifty-one years old. His belated discovery of his talent
as a novelist emerged when he was in the process of compiling a
volume of letters designed to serve as models for humble people not
sufficiently educated to be able to write easily and confidently on
those occasions when letters might be called for. He was working on
this collection in 1739—probably writing letter no. 138, entitled "A
Father to a Daughter in Service, on hearing of her Master's attempting her Virtue"—when it occurred to him that he might work up a
complete novel out of a series of letters written by a virtuous servant
girl to her parents in the intervals of dodging her master's attempts
at rape. He remembered a true story of a virtuous servant girl who
eventually married her master after successfully repulsing his more
irregular approaches, and this exemplary combination of prudence
and virtue appealed to him. He dropped his collection of letters, and
embarked at white heat on *Pamela*, Part I of which he finished in a
couple of months.

The original volume of letters was then completed, and published
in 1741, entitled *Letters Written to and for particular friends, Directing the Requisite Style and Forms To be Observed in writing Familiar
Letters.* It is more than a collection of model letters. Some of his
friends, Richardson tells us in his preface,

> are of opinion, that they will answer several good ends, as they may
> not only direct the *forms* requisite to be observed on the most important
> occasions; but, what is more to the purpose, by the rules and instructions
> contained in them, contribute to *mend the heart, and improve the
> understanding.* . . . The writer . . . has endeavoured . . . to inculcate
> the principles of virtue and benevolence; to describe properly, and
> recommend strongly, the social and relative duties; and to place them
> in such practical lights, that the letters may serve for rules to think and
> act by, as well as forms to write after.

The titles of the letters indicate the sort of thing. "To a Father,
against putting a Youth of but moderate Parts to a Profession that
requires more extensive Abilities." "From an Uncle to a Nephew, on
his keeping bad Company, bad Hours, etc., in his Apprenticeship."

"General Rules for agreeable Conversation in a young Man. From a
Father to a Son." "A young Man in Business, to a Father, desiring
Leave to address his Daughter." "From a young Lady to her Father,
acquainting him with a Proposal of Marriage made to her." "The
Father's Answer, on a Supposition, that he approves *not* of the young
Man's Addresses." "A Father to a Son, to dissuade him from the Vice
of drinking to Excess." "A young Woman in Town to her Sister in
the Country, recounting her narrow Escape from a Snare laid for her,
on her first arrival, by a wicked Procuress." "To rebuke an irregular
Address, when it is not thought proper wholly to discourage it." "An
Excuse to a Person who wants to borrow Money." "A Lady to her
Friend, a young Widow Lady, who, having buried a polite and excellent Husband, inclines to marry a less deserving Gentleman, and of
unequal Fortune." There is only one letter that has no moral relevance
at all; that is "A humorous Epistle of neighbourly Occurrences and
News, to a Bottle-Companion abroad," and here we see Richardson
trying his hand at something rather in the Lovelace manner. Some of
the letters almost sketch out an incipient plot, but the plan of the book
does not allow Richardson to pause long enough over any situation
to develop it into a story. But clearly he was itching to do so.

*   *   *

Richardson's volume of model letters reveals, or at least suggests,
the moral world in which his novels take place. It is a world in which
relationships are of the first importance: the relation between master
and servant, between parents and children, between debtor and credi-
tor, between suitor and sought—these and other relationships condition what is proper in human behaviour, and they are all, in some
sense, symbolic of the relationship between man and God. They reveal
a nexus of rights and duties, the rights being parental and proprietary,
the duties being filial and, in a sense, feudal. Interspersed with the
letters revealing, and indeed commanding, these rights and duties, are
calls to repentance and amendment addressed to those who have gone
astray. We thus have both the Law and the Prophets. The rewards for
duty well done are clearly defined; they are both earthly and heavenly.
Family and social relationships in this world being a microcosm of
the larger relationship between man and God, there is an obvious
analogy between prosperity in this world (the result of the proper
management of human relationships) and eternal felicity in the next.
The analogy between the two worlds is, throughout Richardson's
work, complex but consistent. One moves into the next world only if
the present world fails one. Pamela was able to combine prudence with
virtue and, literally, make the best of both worlds. The title of the
novel is *Pamela: or, Virtue Rewarded.* Clarissa, cheated out of
prudence, fails to secure earthly prosperity but is instead rewarded

in Heaven. I have already suggested that Richardson manipulated
such ideas as prudence and virtue, gentility and morality, with considerable subtlety. Prudence guarantees earthly happiness, while virtue
guarantees heavenly happiness, and the truly fortunate are those to
whom circumstances allow both. Respectability is the outward and
visible sign of prudence, and often, but not always, of true virtue.
(Clarissa loses her external respectability while fully preserving her
true virtue.) Similarly, gentility is the social behaviour and the conventions within which virtue is likely to flourish but does not necessarily flourish. *Clarissa* shows that otherworldliness is not a virtue
until this world has failed one. Good management, economy, methodical disposition of one's time, prudence and efficiency in managing
property and business are important qualities in all Richardson's
heroes and heroines; Clarissa has them all at first, and, though Lovelace
cheats her into the imprudent act of going off with him, she retains
them to the end, changing only the objects to which she applies them:
she gets ready for death with exemplary efficiency, even ordering and
paying for her coffin in advance. It might well be asked whether
Richardson is playing fair in endowing his heroines also with inimita-
ble beauty. What has beauty to do with moral patterns he is tracing?
The answer, I think, is simply that beauty is dangerous; it is more difficult to be virtuous with beauty than without it, because beauty attracts
impure desire and provokes outrage. If, therefore, like Pamela, one
can combine prudence, virtue and beauty, one is truly secure in both
worlds. If, like Clarissa, one has virtue and beauty but is cheated by
the devil out of the exercise of prudence on one critical occasion,
one can compensate by raising virtue to the level of saintliness and,
confident of the next world, cheerfully repudiate this one. Pamela is
held up for our imitation (though Richardson makes it very clear that
only a most exceptionally gifted servant can hope to marry her mas
ter), Clarissa for our adoration. The latter's is the true saint's life.

Richardson's epistolary method was not only a natural one for him,
and an inevitable one in view of the road by which he approached
the novel; it was also the appropriate one for a novelist concerned
with the moment-to-moment recording of the fluctuations of emotion
in the midst of moral struggle. It serves a similar purpose to that of
the soliloquy in drama and the so-called stream of consciousness technique in modern fiction. We are brought immediately and directly
into the consciousness of the character. It is, of course, a convention,
in itself no better and no worse than other conventions in fiction.
There is no point in speculating on how the characters could possibly
have found time to write their hundreds of thousands of words, or
how they could have had the presence of mind, in the midst of so much
anguish, to sit down to write out everything, recalling every word
spoken by themselves and by those with whom they have conversed;

nor should we be distressed to find that they managed even to make copies of their letters and send them to other correspondents, and to transcribe other people's letters to them, and send them around. That Lovelace, rake and daredevil and man of action, impatient of delay and control, should in his turn find both the time and the inclination to write to his friend in the most intimate detail all his nefarious designs against Clarissa, and give a play-by-play account of everything he and she do and say, is of course improbable, but this kind of improbability does not touch the level of probability on which the novel moves. Quite apart from the fact that in the eighteenth century people wrote letters oftener and in more detail than could be imagined in our own age, there is the basic fact that all art requires conventions, and the criterion to be applied is the degree to which the author's use of the convention enables him to build up the proper life in the work. The letters do indeed take the reader into the heart of the developing situation and enable him to follow with extraordinary immediacy the psychological implications of the working out of the moral pattern.

One great difference there is between the epistolary technique and the stream of consciousness method: the latter emphasizes the privateness, the uniqueness, of individual experience, and is therefore appropriate for novels in which the essential loneliness of the individual is stressed and the possibility of adequate communication between individuals is a major problem (as it is, for example, in the novels of Virginia Woolf). The great theme of the eighteenth and often of the nineteenth century novelist is the relation between gentility and virtue; that of the modern novelist is the relationship between loneliness and love. The former theme requires a more public kind of elaboration than is appropriate for the latter, and letters are a most effective way of publicizing private experience. Publicity is important for Richardson. For him, virtue is not a matter between oneself and God; it must be publicly known and admired. Clarissa's death scene, for example, is most carefully staged; it is a device for demonstrating saintliness in action. For the saint to arrange such a demonstration implies a certain degree of self-approval, but that was no problem for Richardson, for whom self-approval must always co-exist with virtue, even with modesty. Clarissa is humble, yet she is full of conscious superiority, which she expresses quite unaffectedly, and the same can be said of Sir Charles Grandison. The moral life is a public life; it is an *exemplum,* something to be seen, approved and imitated or at least admired. Martyrdom would be useless if no one knew of it, and the exemplary life could not be exemplary if no one observed it. Clarissa represents the former, Pamela the latter.

Pamela, which came out in 1740 (though dated 1741), is an altogether simpler novel than *Clarissa.* Its theme is a folk theme, but the

treatment is very different from anything one will find in folk literature. The class background is far from being the simple one of low-
born maiden and high-born lord. Richardson's class was committed
to the view that worth depended on individual effort rather than on
status, yet they were fascinated by status and could not help admiring
and envying it. This gives an ironic ambivalence to the whole moral
pattern of the novel. Squire B. is bent first on seduction and then on
rape; he is dishonest, malevolent, cruel and persecuting. He does everything he can to get Pamela into his physical power, and at one stage is
on the point of committing rape when Pamela providentially falls
into fits and scares him off. (All the while the horrible Mrs Jewkes,
the housekeeper to whom Mr B. had entrusted Pamela in the hope of
softening her up for seduction, looks on with glee and exhorts her
master not to "stand dilly dallying" but to get the act of violation over
with at once. Likewise, in *Clarissa,* the rape of the heroine is watched
and encouraged by Mrs Sinclair and her band of trollops. Even rape
must be public in Richardson.) Yet, after Mr B. has relented and sent
Pamela home, she returns voluntarily when he sends for her, loving
and admiring him all the time, though disapproving of his attempts
to dishonour her. Whenever he relaxes his attempts for a moment, she
is all respect and admiration for him; and when he finally convinces
her that her continued successful resistance has led him to offer marriage, she is all humble love and passionate gratitude. Successful resistance turns lust to love; once Squire B. has got over his weakness
for seduction and rape he is seen by Richardson as a wholly admirable person, not only worthy of the love of a virtuous girl like Pamela
but deserving of her humblest obedience and veneration. She considers
herself unworthy of him. "My good master," she writes,

> my kind friend, my generous benefactor, my worthy protector, and oh!
> all the good words in one, my affectionate husband, that is soon to be
> (be curbed in, my proud heart, know thyself, and be conscious of thy
> unworthiness!) has just left me, with the kindest, tenderest expressions,
> and gentlest behaviour that ever blest a happy maiden.

If a man is a wealthy landowner, and handsome and graceful in manners to boot, he must be considered wholly good so long as he is not
being actively bad. Printers do not become angels by merely ceasing to
threaten girls with sexual violence, but evidently squires do. Richardson, of course, would have been horrified by such a comment. He
claimed that he was showing a genuine reformation of character,
wrought by Pamela's virtue in a young man who had the advantage
of an excellent moral grounding in childhood. But we know better,
and I suspect Pamela did.

This counter pattern which crosses the moral pattern which Richardson consciously planned for the work does not, of course, spoil the

novel; on the contrary, it makes it richer and truer. Human nature is like that; motivation is complex, and the relation between our moral professions and the full psychological explanation of our actions is far from simple. Sometimes it almost seems that Richardson knew this and was deliberately writing a sly, ironic novel. After Mr B.'s first attempts on her, before she has been deceitfully carried off to the country house where Mrs Jewkes presides, Pamela very properly decides to go home to her parents and leave the scene of temptation; but she finds excuse after excuse for not going, and postpones her departure until Mr B. has managed to mature his plan for tricking her into going instead to the house he has waiting for her. And though she professes to prefer honest poverty to vicious luxury, she makes it quite clear in her letters home that she has grown used to a much better way of life than they can afford in their humble cottage. She notes all the fine clothes given her by her late mistress and her master, and, having completed an inventory of what she has, noting what she can in conscience retain, makes such remarks as:

> Here is a calico night-gown, that I used to wear o'mornings. 'Twill be rather too good for me when I get home; but I must have something. . . . And here are four other shifts, one the fellow to that I have on; another pretty good one, and the other two old fine ones, that will serve me to turn and wind with at home, for they are not worth leaving behind me; and here are two pairs of shoes; I have taken the lace off, which I will burn, and may-be will fetch me some little matter at a pinch, with an old silver buckle or two.

Most suggestive of all, she gives up the fine clothes her lady had given her, determined not to sail under false colours, and provides herself with a new, simpler outfit.

> And so when I had dined, up stairs I went, and locked myself up in my little room. There I dressed myself in my new garb, and put on my round-eared ordinary cap, but with a green knot, my home-spun grown and petticoat, and plain leather shoes, but yet they are what they call Spanish leather; and my ordinary hose, ordinary I mean to what I have been lately used to, though I should think good yarn may do very well for every day, when I come home. A plain muslin tucker I put on, and my black silk necklace, instead of the French necklace my lady gave me; and put the ear-rings out of my ears. When I was quite equipped, I took my straw hat in my hand, with its two blue strings, and looked in the glass, as proud as any thing. To say truth, I never liked myself so well in my life.
>
> O the pleasure of descending with ease, innocence, and resignation!— Indeed, there is nothing like it! An humble mind, I plainly see, cannot meet with any very shocking disappointment, let Fortune's wheel turn round as it will.

And down she trips, looking, as she very well knows, more ravishing than ever, and runs straight into her master, who pretends not to recognize the "pretty neat damsel."

> He came up to me, and took me by the hand, and said, "Whose pretty maiden are you? I dare say you are Pamela's sister, you are so like her. So neat, so clean, so pretty! Why, child, you far surpass your sister, Pamela!"
> I was all confusion, and would have spoken, but he took me about the neck: "Why," said he, "you are very pretty, child: I would not be so free with your *sister,* you may believe; but I must kiss *you.*"—"O Sir," said I, "I am Pamela, indeed I am: indeed I am Pamela, *her ownself!*"

This, and scenes like this, are admirably done, whatever Richardson thought he was really doing. It is as though Richardson knows Pamela so well that he has simply to let himself *be* Pamela in order to write the letters. He does not have to understand her or to analyse her motives, any more than she understands and analyses herself. She sets herself out to attract her master from the beginning, though she herself does not realize it and perhaps her creator does not; but prudence as well as morality demands that she keep herself unravished while keeping his interest in her at fever pitch. She thinks she is trying to escape his clutches, but allows herself to be deflected from her attempts at escape by the slightest obstacles (even to the point of supposing an inoffensive cow to be a fierce bull), and when he finally lets her go she flies back to him at his summons.

When he releases her, she leaves with a reluctance that surprises herself. "I think I was loth to leave the house. Can you believe it?—What could be the matter with me, I wonder? I felt something so strange at my heart! I wonder what ailed me." She writes home in this troubled state of mind from a village where the coach has paused. "Here I am, at a little poor village, almost such a one as yours!" The smallness and poverty of the village (and by implication of her parents' home) are mentioned more than once. And when Mr B.'s letter arrives, asking her to return (though only in the most oblique way promising marriage) she writes in her journal, "O my exulting heart!" She knows now what she has wanted all along.

The rest of Part I and all of Part II are much less interesting. The marriage duly takes place, and there is a lively scene a little while afterwards when, the Squire being temporarily away from home, his sister Lady Davers calls and, assuming that Pamela is her brother's mistress and not his wife, abuses her with fine snobbish scorn. But after this the book swells into a chorus of admiration from the neighbouring gentry. Pamela's story is known, and she is trotted around aristocratic drawing-rooms to be admired for her successful defence of her chastity and her nobility of character. She has perfect manners, and conducts herself everywhere with model decorum. Lady Davers is reconciled and joins the chorus of admiration. One of Pamela's last acts in Part I is to exercise her benevolence on an illegitimate daughter of her adoring husband, product of an early and fully confessed amour.

Part II, added in 1742, to replace and discredit continuations (both serious and satirical) by other hands, is a dull marriage manual showing the ideal couple in action, with a mild and temporary break in perfect felicity when Squire B. becomes involved with a widowed countess at a masked ball. (Thus showing the immorality of masked balls, which Richardson was never tired of preaching.) Pamela becomes the oracle, dispensing wisdom in her letters on everything from the state of the drama to Locke's views on education. The most interesting part of *Pamela* is over by the time her marriage is accomplished.

Pamela is thus a psychologically realistic fairy tale grounded in middle class morality which achieves a level of ironic counterstatement by the sheer honesty and accuracy of its heroine's self-revelation. Mr B. is less successful than the heroine; Richardson had little first-hand knowledge of the manners and conversation of the higher squirearchy and nobility, and Mr B. is interesting only for the reactions he produces in Pamela. It has long been the fashion to complain about the morality of the book, with its attempt to reconcile virtue with material self-interest. But what is wrong with reconciling virtue with self-interest if you can? There are three factors involved: what you are really like (psychology); what will get you success in this life (prudence); what will get you success in the next life and may with luck also do so in this (virtue). Pamela is true to her psychology (as one might say) and manipulates her virtue into prudence with unconscious art. (One assumes that it is unconscious.) All one can say is: nice work if you can get it.

There is surely nothing immoral in refusing to have sexual relations with the man you are in love with until marriage secures you a permanent relationship with him. It is not *that* which seems to me the moral flaw in the novel. What I object to is something that appears equally clearly in *Clarissa,* namely Richardson's narrow and mechanical view of sex, and indeed of love. Pamela's love for Squire B. cannot be easily dissociated from her admiration of his position and wealth; once he has been prevailed on to behave decently his position and wealth can be allowed to make him desirable. It is not that Square B. marries Pamela because he cannot satisfy his lust outside marriage; it is rather that her continued defence of her chastity, and his reading of her letters and journal, have aroused in him a moral admiration of her character which changes his sexual desire into moral approval. Sex, wherever it is treated in Richardson, is presented as something violent and violating. The notion of mutual sexual satisfaction never seems to have occurred to him. None of Richardson's rakes seeks such satisfaction; they want to rape; they are not sensualists but competitive collectors of virginities by violence. In *Clarissa*, Lovelace achieves his nefarious purpose on a drugged and passive victim. It is a purely quantitative business, a matter of arithmetic: the more people you can violate, the greater your glory as a rake. This is a Kinsey report view of sex, a mechanical as well as an unrealistic view. And the rake's view of sex as violence done by the man to the woman is lower even than Kinsey. The woman is sacrificed to male violence, and even marriage but provides the proper arena for such a sacrifice. In *Clarissa* images of the victim stretched out before the knife recur again and again, directly and obliquely. In *Sir Charles Grandison* the wedding night of the hero and heroine is described in terms suggestive of the bride as a sacrifice. Richardson understood the housemaid's quiver of joy at the thought of marrying her handsome master, and reproduces this kind of sensibility with great brilliance. But that has as little to do either with sex or with love as has the attitude of his rakes, for whom a seduction or a rape (it is all one to them) is, like climbing Mount Everest, a matter of planning and stamina. There is no pleasure in it: the pleasure lies in the satisfaction of having done it. One can, if one likes, relate this characteristic of Richardson's to the Puritan suspicion of sex, but I for one am dissatisfied with such easy generalizations. Many Puritans, because of their very suspicion of sex perhaps, had an uncanny insight into its nature and working. I suspect it has something to do with Richardson's own temperament and history.

Samuel Richardson: *"Pamela"*

by Alan D. McKillop

Richardson was fifty years old when he changed the course of English fiction by writing and publishing *Pamela*. . . . [It] was published in two volumes in November, 1740; an inferior continuation, into which Richardson was forced by the appearance of a spurious sequel, appeared in December, 1741. *Pamela I* enjoyed a popular success comparable to that of *The Beggar's Opera* or Hogarth's prints, though many people thought of the book as on the outer fringe of literature. As far as we can tell, there had been nothing quite like this *réclame* before; *Pamela* at its inception was "low" in subject matter and style, and the "low" in literature, it was thought, needed clear justification. If a plain or "low" work was written as a record of miscellaneous adventure, as a deliberate literary burlesque, or as a piece of humble piety for low or middling people, one could understand that, but *Pamela* did not fit neatly into any of these categories. Even in our own day, people who would never think of evaluating contemporary fiction in terms of subject matter are content to smile pityingly at the report of a servant girl, graceful, demure, and conventionally virtuous and pious, who is the victim of some extraordinarily clumsy attempts at seduction on the part of her young master Mr. B——, but who sincerely or shrewdly holds out for marriage, and thus wins her man. It is a simple and popular plot, with many analogues, and not without precedent in the society of Richardson's day. . . . The Earl of Egmont wrote in his diary for February 4, 1745, that various maidservants and others of low degree had recently married dukes and earls.[1] In a lettter to Hill, Richardson said that he had heard such a story from a friend some years before,[2] and we have seen that he repeated this statement to Stinstra.* But *Pamela* is not a mere story of a *mésalliance,* or merely a scandalous account of the wiles of a would-be seducer, though it com-

---

From *"Samuel Richardson"* by A. D. McKillop. From The Early Masters of English Fiction (*Lawrence, Kansas: University of Kansas Press, 1956*), *pp. 51, 55–63. Copyright © 1956 by the University of Kansas Press. Reprinted in abridged form by permission of the publisher.*

[1] *Diary of the Earl of Egmont,* III (1923), 307–8. Hist. MSS Comm.

[2] *Correspondence of Samuel Richardson* [1804], I, lxix–lxxiii.

* [In a letter quoted earlier in the chapter (McKillop. *The Early Masters,* p. 49).]

bines the two familiar themes in its own way. Neither is it merely a Puritan conduct-book, or a manifesto of middle-class piety. Richardson wrote it *con amore*, the subject kindling his interest.

> While I was writing the two volumes, my worthy-hearted wife, and the young lady who is with us, when I had read them some part of the story, which I had begun without their knowing it, used to come in to my little closet every night, with—"Have you any more of Pamela, Mr. R.? We are come to hear a little more of Pamela," &c. This encouraged me to prosecute it, which I did so diligently, through all my other business, that by a memorandum on my copy, I began it Nov. 10, 1739, and finished it Jan. 10, 1739–40. And I have often, censurable as I might be thought for my vanity for it, and lessening to the taste of my two female friends, had the story of Moliere's Old Woman in my thoughts upon the occasion.[3]

Richardson's term "enlargement" ** gives us the key, along with another favorite phrase of his, "writing to the moment." The presentation of a situation in letter form suggested the idea of changing the scale of the narrative by giving a minutely particular account of thoughts, actions, and accompanying circumstances at such frequent intervals as to make up a current record rather than a retrospective summary. There is a connection or parallel here with English empirical philosophy, with its emphasis on the primary value of immediate experience from one conscious moment to another, and this connection is later elaborated and made explicit by Sterne.[4] But it would be pretentious to tie up Richardson closely with epistemology; an alert literary intelligence might "write to the moment" without going to school to the philosophers. Chaucer centuries before had noted the unrealized possibility of fiction on such a scale.

> Now, perhaps, some one may expect me to recount every word, message, glance, or expression that Troilus used in communicating with his dear mistress. That would be a long story, to describe all the words and looks of a man in such a difficult situation. To tell the truth, neither I nor anyone else ever heard of such a thing being done, and even though I wanted to do it, I couldn't: a single one of their letters might be half as large as this book. The writer I am following didn't choose to put such a document on record—how then should I be expected to write a line of it? (*Troilus*, III, 491–504)

[3] *Ibid.*, I, lxxiv–lxxv. Richardson probably got the reference to Molière's "Old Woman" from *Spectator* No. 70.

** [Elsewhere in the chapter, Richardson is quoted explaining the genesis of the novel: " 'Little did I think,' he wrote to Aaron Hill, 'of making one, much less two volumes of it.' But he thought such a simple story might turn the young from 'the pomp and parade of romance-writing' and 'might tend to promote the cause of religion and virtue. . . . I therefore gave way to enlargement: and so Pamela became as you see her.' " (*The Early Masters*, p. 54.)]

[4] See below [McKillop, *The Early Masters*], pp. 193–196.

And Cervantes evidently felt that a vast circumstantial narrative needed the defense his playful commentary could supply:

> In very truth, all who enjoy stories like this should show their gratitude to Cide Hamete, its first author, for his meticulousness in recording its minutest details, leaving nothing, however trivial, which he does not bring clearly to light. He depicts thoughts, reveals intentions, answers unspoken questions, clears up doubts, in fact elucidates the slightest points the most captious critic could raise. O most renowned author! [5]

Dostoevsky puts the novelist's double program of inclusion and exclusion with characteristic directness and simplicity: "But I see I can't go on like this, partly because some things I did not hear, others I did not notice, and others I have forgotten, but most of all because, as I have said before, I have literally no time or space to mention everything that was said and done." [6] And Stendhal asks with similar directness, "How am I to find space for all the arguments, all the ways of looking at what was happening to him which, for three mortal hours on end, kept this impassioned man in torment?" [7]

The details in both Defoe and Richardson always bear more or less directly on the question of what the central character is to do in a given situation, but this situation is presented in more complex terms in Richardson, and there is more careful subordination of external detail and incident. Thus when Goodman Andrews sets out to discover the truth about his daughter:

> He put on a clean Shirt and Neckcloth, (which he brought in his Pocket) at an Alehouse there, and got shav'd; and so, after he had eat some Bread and Cheese, and drank a Can of Ale, he set out for my Master's House, with a heavy Heart, dreading for me, and in much fear of being brow-beaten. He had, it seems, asked at the Alehouse, what Family the 'Squire had down here, in hopes to hear something of me; and they said, A Housekeeper, two Maids, and, at present, two Coachmen, and two Grooms, a Footman, and a Helper. Was that all? he said. They told him, there was a young Creature there, belike, who *was, or was to be,* his Mistress, or somewhat of that nature; but had been his Mother's Waiting-maid. This, he said, grieved his Heart, and confirmed his Fears.[8]

We note the lists of items, as in Defoe, but Defoe would have given the inquiries at greater length; and Fielding might have given a longer alehouse scene. Richardson gets on to what is for him the main point— the confrontation of Mr. B— and Goodman Andrews, and the old

---

[5] *Don Quixote*, II, xl. Trans. I. M. Cohen (Penguin Classics), p. 721.

[6] *The Brothers Karamazov*, IV, xii, 1. Trans. Constance Garnett (Modern Library), p. 803.

[7] *The Charterhouse of Parma*, chap. vii. Trans. C. K. Scott-Moncrieff (New York, n.d.), p. 171.

[8] *Pamela* (Shakespeare Head Edition), II, 67–68. All references below to Richardson's novels are to this edition, unless otherwise indicated.

man's attempt to grasp and interpret what Mr. B— says to him. Dialogue and "air and manner" are important as clues to the attitudes and reactions of other people. As Richardson's heroine Clarissa says at the beginning of her story: "And then you will always have me give you minute descriptions, nor suffer me to pass by the air and manner in which things are spoken that are to be taken notice of; rightly observing, that air and manner often express more than the accompanying words" (I, 8). His "minute descriptions" are selective. His way of "writing to the moment" is not indiscriminate expansion of descriptive detail, but running record of significant circumstance and fluctuating feeling from the point of view of the letter-writer.

Such a record gives the reader a continuous and cumulative impression of living through the experience, and thus creates a new kind of sympathy with the character whose experiences are being shared. It is not merely that the character's feelings and observations are systematically presented; this in itself might, and sometimes does, lead to a tedious and trivial record. The point is that here we have the close linking of memory and current impression with anticipation of what is to come—a future not merely conceived as ultimate outcome—will Pamela's chastity be violated? will the story end with wedding bells?—but a future emerging directly from the spacious present—what is to be done next, whether Pamela is to be sent to Mr. B—'s sister Lady Davers, or home to her parents, whether Mr. B— is to marry someone else, whether Pamela might be married off to the chaplain Mr. Williams, whether Mr. B—, as Pamela is warned, plans to entrap her by a mock-marrage. One question about the immediate future leads to another, and we get a very close *liaison des scènes*. For example, if Pamela is about to go home to her parents, what clothes shall she wear? This leads to the "rustic garb" scene, a very skilful performance, in which minor details point back to significant major tensions. Richardson is not afraid to reiterate the minor questions; when he is at his best he is not concerned with asking himself how they would sound in a pulpit or a drawing room.

It is just this resolution not to exclude the apparently undignified or trivial that marks Richardson's art. Defoe is concerned with such questions of policy too, but he does not steadily elaborate them within what we may call the domestic milieu. Naturally Richardson's procedure was not described in this way in the 1740's; those who were fascinated by the book could perhaps give less adequate explanations than those who were vexed by it. There was sometimes a combination of irritation and fascination which appears with particular clearness in the French comments, but contemporary criticism was on the whole inarticulate and inadequate. Contemporary readers did not oblige posterity by saying the right things. *Pamela* could be called low, hypocritical, tedious, at times indecent. Much of the discussion is carried on in terms of formal piety, material goods, and literal physical chastity. Richardson of course deliberately adopts a plain colloquial style for Pamela's reports, and he forgoes many things that might seem to be of advantage to the novelist. Pamela is isolated, first at the Bedfordshire estate of her master and then at his Lincolnshire estate, where she is kept prisoner at Mr. B—'s orders. The rest of the cast is made up of Mr. B—and a few servants and dependents, the good Mrs. Jervis, the bad Mrs. Jewkes, the inept but well-meaning Parson Williams. Pamela's mistress, Mr. B—'s mother, is dead; if she had lived she would have complicated the plot considerably, but affairs are worked out between Mr. B— and Pamela before his family, in the person of his redoubtable sister Lady Davers, asserts itself. Richardson gives us glimpses of the English household of his time, but it is not one of his primary purposes to do so, and in *Pamela* he deliberately avoids the presentation of a full family circle. He does not devise a wide range of episodes, but works out his effects from a few simple premises. Such devices as sending the characters on a circumstantially reported journey, or putting the central character in London or Bath, to watch the people go by, are not for him. Nor does he allow Pamela's parents, to whom her letters and journals are directed, to take effective action; in fact, he artificially limits outside intervention.

On the positive side, Richardson cultivates intensively the area he covers, and the letter form is a means to this end. In *Pamela* he follows a simple plan: the "narratist" sends letters or keeps a journal, but does not regularly receive and answer letters. Why, we may ask, should not this account have been presented as simple narrative in the first person? The letter convention emphasizes the medium and the method, and may be open to the objection that it is clumsy and ostentatious, that it obtrudes itself on the attention somewhat to the same effect as an elaborate story in a news-weekly about its wonderful method of getting news, or a television show about the marvels of producing a television show. Documents must be provided at any cost, and readers have smiled at Pamela's indomitable determination to write, even when there seems to be little prospect that anyone will read what she has written, even when correspondence has been cut off and she has to hide supplies of writing materials. And in the same way Richardson's heroine Clarissa says, "I must write on, altho' I were not to send it to anybody" (III, 221). As developed in *Clarissa* the system requires not only indefatigable correspondents but servants who devote much of their time to carrying letters. When letters cannot be written or sent immediately, the character may be occupied in keeping a journal or in making minutes, rough notes, and memoranda. And as I have said elsewhere, "The writing of the letters is only the beginning; they are copied, sent, received, shown about, discussed, answered, even perhaps hidden, intercepted, stolen, altered, or forged." Endless variations are possible here: thus when Clarissa expects her room to be searched by her family, she leaves in view a letter "which affording arguments suitable to my case, may chance (thus accidentally to be fallen upon) to incline them to favour me" (II, 330).

In *Pamela* the variations on the letter form are comparatively simple. Without going into full detail, we may note that when Mr. B— at last gets a chance to read Pamela's journal entire, he recalls her after he has given her full permission, her trials now over, to return to her parents; thus not only the earlier action but the record of the earlier action and the analysis and reception of that record condition the story. The writing of the novel is part of the action of the novel.[9]

If *Pamela* had been merely a Puritan conduct-book it would now be forgotten, like Defoe's *Family Instructor*. In writing his continuation of the story Richardson discovered that his analysis of a situation after it had become static ended in listless verbosity, and that the defect could not be remedied by drawing on conduct-books and collections of commonplaces concerning education, family life, and other social relationships. An added complication was that he now wanted to retreat from the radical democracy implicit in *Pamela I;* the original case of the virtuous serving maid does not fit easily into the accepted view of society set forth in *Pamela II.* And yet *Pamela II* gave Richardson valuable experience and taught him the danger of relying on miscellaneous letters. In the desire to elevate Pamela's style and in the plan to keep her writing long letters at any cost, Richardson may have been influenced from an early stage by the educational theory of polite correspondence which I have already mentioned;[***] such a theory was probably necessary to get him beyond the brief and meager models of the epistolary manuals. No matter how spontaneous and independent an artist is, he cannot dispense entirely with preconceived doctrine about genre and style. The peril was that such preconceptions might have checked Richardson's development. He and his daughters came to be somewhat ashamed of the "low" style of *Pamela I.*

Yet it was *Pamela I* that was the great success, and the success was popular rather than literary. There were dramatizations, Pamela poems, spurious continuations and imitations, waxworks, pictures, fans, as well as derisive comments on Pamela's virtue by Fielding and others, but these matters need not detain us here, save as affording full illustration of the phenomenon of the best seller. *Pamela* never became

---

[9] For further discussion of Richardson's use of the letter form see Ernest A. Baker, *The History of the English Novel* (1924–31), IV, 22–24; Godfrey F. Singer, *The Epistolary Novel* (Philadelphia, 1933); Frank G. Black, *The Epistolary Novel in the Late Eighteenth Century* (Eugene, 1940), University of Oregon Monographs: Studies in Literature and Philology, No. 2; Alan D. McKillop, "Epistolary Technique in Richardson's Novels," *Rice Institute Pamphlet,* XXXVIII (1951), 36–54.

[***] [Earlier in the chapter (McKillop, *The Early Masters,* p. 55).]

a universal book like *Robinson Crusoe,* but aroused more immediate excitement with an appeal to sex and sentimental democracy; Upton Sinclair has recently recaptured in part the spirit in which the book was first received by imitating it sympathetically in *Another Pamela: or Virtue Still Rewarded* (1950). An unusual contemporary example of what we may call mature and yet spontaneous literary criticism of *Pamela* appears in an early letter of Richard Hurd's:

> I thank you, good Sir, a thousand times for recommending Pamela to me. I had some how conceiv'd such an unaccountable prejudice agst: it, that nothing less than your good Opinion could have induc'd me to read it. But what a treasure of Beauties had I then lost! to say the least of a work, of wch. the most one can say is too little, I never saw Nature in such perfection before. I make no scruple to say there never were any characters more justly drawn, with greater propriety & exactness, or of a more glowing likeness to the life. The whole is literally a speaking Picture, & by reason of the several distressful Incidents, that are work'd up in it, as moving a one as ever did credit to any pencil. As a draught of Nature then I must read, love, & admire it, & stand amaz'd that any Reader of Taste should hazard his reputation so much as to own a dislike of it. But in it's moral capacity I am not so positive. On the other hand I incline to suspect more danger from it to the generality of young readers, than advantage. M^{r}. B's character is a little too engaging to make a Debauchee sufficiently distasteful to the youth of his quality & fortune; & the very nature, that strikes so much in Pamela's narrative of her own distresses is, I fear, still more dangerous to most female Fancies. 'Tis hazardous, nay I'll go further 'tis hurtful to paint Nature in such cases too faithfully. The too lively representation warms & inflames—the passions kindle at the view, & want more than the fair complainants ejaculations, & reflections to cool them again. This, Sir, I cannot but fear will be the probable consequence of some part of Pamela's charming Journal to the unconfirm'd virtuous of both Sexes. I mention it not as an Objection to the work, (for I am satisfy'd 'tis the very perfection of it) but as a hindrance to it's moral Design. 'Twill be a pleasure to find myself mistaken, & too apprehensive in this point, for 'tis with reluctance I observe anything in the lovely piece, that may keep it from being generally read.[10]

But the immediate effect of the book might appear to be a mere vogue or craze: there was little formal literary endorsement or support. The more important direct results of *Pamela,* indeed, appeared in *Joseph Andrews* and *Clarissa.*

[10] British Museum Addit. MS 32,557, f. 47. Richard Hurd to Cox Macro, November 7, 1742.

Justice to *Pamela*

by B. L. Reid

Well my story, surely, would furnish out a surprising kind of novel, if well told.
                                        —Pamela

After staggering for years under a weight of fame greater than he should ever have been asked to support, Samuel Richardson fell, it seems, and for a long time now he has lain kicking feebly in the dust of literary history. His novels, great in size and in some of their achievements, have joined that honorable list of virtually unvisited monuments of English fiction that includes, unhappily, *Bleak House, Middlemarch, Moby Dick, The Marble Faun, The Wings of the Dove,* and *Finnegans Wake.* Their wing of the museum has faithful attendants but few paid admissions, it is kept open by subsidy. Outside, in the open air of literary give and take, those few cubits that are spent on Richardson's *Pamela* are full of cloudy nonsense. I should like to lament that state of things and do what I can to change it. . . . What I hope to do is to draw up a defence against the two commonest and most serious indictments of the novel: that it is fatally sentimental and artificial, and that its pretentious moralism is vicious and false. . . .

My notion that *Pamela* is a novel of striking verisimilitude is by no means wholly heterodox, yet I think that emphasis in the received opinion . . . runs largely the other way. This seems to be a kind of standard schematic line of literary historians: Richardson is progenitor of the sentimental novel, not the realistic novel; he is a captive of Puritan theology, hence a slave to all the violent special pleading and distortion of view that that dogma enjoins; he is a creature circumscribed by all the paraphernalia of middle-class sensibility—a shopkeeper with a shopkeeper's ethics and a shopkeeper's aesthetics; Richardson had to be satirized before we would have realism—the realistic tradition in the English novel begins with Fielding and *Joseph Andrews,* an avowed satire on *Pamela.* . . .

Actually the scheme seems to me substantially but crudely accurate, so my quarrel here is a gentle one, not with the substance of the historians' line but with its crudity. The historian does *Pamela* very serious injustice if he encourages the schoolboy to tick the novel off as *merely* sententious, sentimental, tiresomely moralistic, stiffly artificial, and hopelessly prolix (and so obviously unreadable). There is truth in all these epithets, but still they do not contain Pamela, or explain her. Her story, I insist, is funny, it is touching, it is endlessly interesting, and beyond all these it is finally convincing: it grows true and actual. In spite of all its confessed vices, the novel does possess a dense and considerable verisimilitude. That is really all I want to argue at this point—that *Pamela* has a kind of residual realism that is much larger and more conclusive than critics like to admit: that it is a credible incredibility, a real unreality.

There is much that is patently unreal in *Pamela,* and we should begin by noticing its worst sins of falseness to life. These occur mainly in habits of style and of characterization. Thus the high rhetorical polish of the novel's utterance, its glossy surface and its elegant periodic undulation of syntactical movement—both beautiful and dull —is completely incredible as the epistolary style of a fifteen-year-old country girl. No servant girl, and no fifteen-year-old miss of any station, ever talked like this. I do not refer to her flux or her redundancy —which seem to me functional, charming and believable—but to her vocabulary, her range of reference, and her sentence structure, the general hand-rubbed finish of the discourse. Her rhetoric is superb, but in terms of character it is also absurd. The book is one long unbroken example of what I mean, and it is not even necessary to quote to prove the point.

Richardson's characterization, or rather his caricaturing of character, is a still more nagging flaw in his realism. Pamela, if we look at her only as she functions in the novel's tiresome moral line, is one-dimensional to paper-thinness; she is madly Puritanical, really a maniac of virtue. In a different direction Mrs. Jewkes and Lady Davers are also caricatures, character-absolutes of much crudeness in the conception, though undeniably, too, of an almost Dickensian gusto and impetus. Mr. B., while he is at least conventionally satisfactory as the baffled rake, is in no way convincing as the complacent husband— "palpably uxorious" was Milton's resonant phrase in another context for such behavior:

> . . . let me tell my sweet girl, that, after having been long tossed by the boisterous winds of a more culpable passion, I have now conquered it, and am not so much the victim of your beauty, all charming as you are, as of your virtue: and therefore may more boldly promise for myself, having so stable a foundation for my affection, which, should this outward beauty fail, will increase with your virtue, and shine forth

the brighter, as that is more illustriously displayed by the augmented opportunities your future condition will afford you.

"O the dear charming man," burbles Pamela; but the reader sees too plainly that his outright transformation is shoddily motivated and ridiculously complete. His absurd *gravitas* and airs of old age at twenty-six make him not a legitimately altered character but simply an unfamiliar man. Thus Professor Cross was surely right when he said there was in Richardson "a lingering on of one form of allegory." But again this seems to be but a crude truth, and while it will carry us through a hurried paraphrase, it will by no means carry us to the real boundaries of the novel.

We may try, surrounded by Richardson's imperfections, to classify the means by which he converts the complex unreality of his subject, his form, and his personages into a reality considerable enough to catch, hold, and delight our attention. In order that we may not stupidly recapitulate the allegorist's emphatic error, let us remember now that reality is not absolute, not one but many. We may call for aid from a canonized realist, Henry James, who thought more often and more wisely about the art of novel than anyone else I know. In his great essay "The Art of Fiction," James said:

> The characters, the situation, which strike one as real will be those that touch and interest one most, but the measure of reality is very difficult to fix. The reality of Don Quixote or of Mr. Micawber is a very delicate shade. . . .

In the same essay James testified to the centrality of the issue:

> . . . the air of reality (solidity of specification) seems to me to be the supreme virtue of a novel—the merit on which all its other merits . . . helplessly and submissively depend. If it be not there they are all as nothing, and if these be there, they owe their effect to the success with which the author has produced the illusion of life.

Reality is multiform and vital, then, and we are right to be interested in what Richardson *makes* us believe.

We see at once that *Pamela*'s persuasiveness is partly a matter of form and structure. In a purely technical sense, realism aside, the novel's worst vices are probably those of dramatic structure: it is too long for its essential work; too inclusive, too unselective; too often static in movement and slack in tension ("I like those great still books," Tennyson said, and wished for one of hundreds of volumes); it reaches its turning point much too early, proportionately, and the falling action is thus far too long and too merely thin and sweet. But if its sins are in part those of structure, so are its virtues. At the simplest level, we feel that the epistolary method itself carries a kind of gratuitous *cachet* of realism. That is, letters are normally vehicles for our common factual doings, a letter presupposes an actual writer and an actual reader, a letter is stiff and undramatic: if one wants to propound a fiction not a truth, why not choose a suppler, more active form? Our prior notions of the normal function of the form subtly if shallowly suggest to us an actual maiden, an actual seducer, and an actual marriage. The effect grows thicker as Richardson manipulates the epistles, the whole familiar machinery of hidden pens and ink and paper and wafers, of evasions and discoveries, of secretings in bosoms and underlinens and sunflowers. Then there is the whole clustering, hovering, lingering effect—later much mulitiplied in *Clarissa*—which comes to surround an incident as it goes its echoic progress in this method: the incident occurs, it is reflected on, committed to paper, committed to a porter, spied upon, received, reflected on, responded to, and perhaps returned to the original actors. The whole complex repercussive effect grows much thicker than the printed page. The epistolary form, too, excuses logically, though it does not justify artistically, much of the buttery smoothness of Pamela's unctuous rhetoric: that is, a letter is an editing of life, not life itself, and has an editor's option to tailor and furbish experience. So Richardson, having once posited a servant maid with flair and flow, can sensibly ask of us some suspension of disbelief—though by no means as full a suspension as he does in fact demand. As one quick instance of the conviction carried so simply by the epistolary form itself, consider the novel's first letter. There the cold plunge *in medias res* with the bald announcement of the death of old Lady B. and the immediate joining of the issue with her son have all the disorderly naïveté of life itself; it is only by hindsight that we see much later that they have as well all the ordered craft of art itself.

One does not know exactly how much verisimilitude to claim for Richardson's handling of the sequence of incident in *Pamela*. It is obvious in the first place that Richardson, in his somewhat fussy feminine way, is endlessly inventive of incident, but his inventiveness is not our present concern. More relevant is the fact that incidents in *Pamela* are likely to be little more than interesting fits of manners: if they are dramatic at all they are so in terms of revelation of personality rather than of deeps of character or morals. Still it seems to me that this admitted manneristic shallowness, while it disappoints our hopes of larger dramatic tension and thematic sweep, should not seriously disappoint our sense of drawing-room and boudoir reality, our humble guesses as to how life is normally conducted in such precious stations as the country-house environment of Mr. B. We should note as well in Richardson's favor that he depends very little —much less than the satire of *Joseph Andrews* implies—on pure coincidence or lucky accident in managing the sequence of incident; the confusing of Mr. B.'s letter to Mrs. Jewkes with that to Pamela is

almost the only case that springs to mind. What is very damaging to
the book's realism, on the other hand, is the stylized balancing of
situations: outrage in the summer house is succeeded by sweet repentance in the summer house; tearful farewells by triumphant re-
unions; vulgar assertiveness by contrite capitulation. All this is much
too meagre, pat, unmotivated—too sentimental, in a word.

But offsetting this distinctly wooden and artificial patterning of
events Richardson offers two additional virtues of structure—a different order of repetition, and a large and noble quality we can best
call modulation. This other simpler repetition is incremental, and it
seems to me quietly hilarious. Instances of it are the superlative-plus
"in England" phrase pattern Richardson is so fond of—bluff, hearty
and in its mingled dullness and good humor wonderfully life like:
"the loveliest girl in England," "the happiest man in England," "the
honestest fellow in England." Or consider Richardson's exquisite fool-
ing with the name of "Miss Sally Godfrey," with Pamela's fixation on
that name like a mannerly lady bulldog once Lady Davers has rashly
pronounced it, until the well-bred tension is all nicely relaxed with
Mr. B.'s manly narrative of the days when he was a very bad boy indeed and his revelation of the sweet consequences of his error in little
Miss Goodwin of the "fine black eye" and "genteel shape." All utterly
phoney, yet still irresistibly affecting and, moreover, acceptable for
the long moment of our reading as purest truth. Best of all in this line
is Mr. B.'s fanatic urge to get his hand into Miss Andrews' cloistered
bosom, where he infallibly blunders on the trigger that sets off her
heroic serial fainting fits. The double fetishism of the maneuver is
high low comedy, and especially in its testimony to masculine single-
mindedness it is uproarious and real.

Now in all of this we may, if we choose, follow those readers who
find Richardson humorless and helplessly moralistic: if we do so we
have to call these and other repetitions nothing more than instances
of slovenliness or sententiousness. But I think they are not so, and
a careful reading of the management of tone and timing in the Sally
Godfrey detail, especially, will show that they are conscious and
delicious art. . . . Richardson did have a comic sense; it was poten-
tially fine, as the Howe-Hickman relationship in *Clarissa* shows. But
his self-conscious moralism told him constantly to depress it, and it
almost seems that it emerges in the novels only when it escaped him
in moments of inattention on the part of his censorious conscience.
All this is an instance, I think, of the curious fact to which we shall
have to return: Richardson is a classic example of a man misreading
himself. He thought he was a great moralist serving his texts in a
merely adequate bolus of fiction; he was in fact a jejune moralist
(not, I shall argue, a dishonest one) but a great shaggy artist who was
prevented by his own moral fatuity and that of his readers from ever

seeing himself in an adequate mirror, currying his coat, and emerging
as the truly first-rate novelist he should have been. In short, it seems
to me we have to deal here with a prime case of *unconscious* genius.
The little tricks I have been mentioning above are minor manifesta-
tions of that fact.

That other softening quality I have called modulation is one not
easy to demonstrate, since it is a property of the book's larger rhythms
and makes itself felt almost unconsciously in the main. By modulation
I mean here the achievement of topography and texture that is various and interesting—rise and fall, shading, ranges of mood and colora-
tion, tension and release; the whole vague but vital matter of subjective flexibility within the objective strait jacket of the epistolary form
and the sentimentality of the theme. My point is that this variety, this
orderly disorder, is the rhythm of life itself and that Richardson commands it skillfully in *Pamela*. Perhaps the best instance is his beautiful control of the slow, faltering, settling movement of Pamela's
descent from the peak of her apprehension to the quiet confidence of
the moment when Mr. B. indeed marries her in an invincibly legal
ceremony in an unquestionable chapel furnished with an undisputable
clergyman. Other cases are the nicely imagined (and startlingly modern) ambivalent pattern of Pamela's love-hate response to Mr. B.
before the marriage, the slow conversion of Lady Davers, the fearful,
delightful reaction of Goodman Andrews to the spectacle of his daughter's good fortune, the broadening and lightening of the comic tone on
the two occasions when the seducer is driven to hiding in the sacred
boudoir. Only three important elements in the novel seem to me
totally lacking in this quality of modulation. One is the character of
the married Mr. B., in which the absence of shading is a fundamental
and very damaging flaw; another is Pamela's love for her parents, and
one neither expects nor wants that to vary; the third is her redundant
piousness: of her piety one cannot quite say that it is incredible—
only that it is dreadfully dull.

After confessing above that the basic principle of characterization
in *Pamela* is allegorical, I suggested that that did not complete the
matter. There is a strong residual reality in Richardson's persons that
notably fleshes out the leanness of allegory. The heroine herself, who
begins by being the most fully allegorical figure, ends by becoming
the most fully human. Beginning in ignorance, one hopes for a time
that Pamela is going to be a satirical figure: as such she would be
quite perfect. But then one concludes, sadly at first, that Richardson
has no satirical intention at all; he wants us to accept Pamela exactly
as she fatally is, in full crushing sobriety—an impregnably Good Girl.
This is disappointing, especially if one has trained on Fielding. But
the thing that interests me now is how Richardson converts one, first,
to acceptance of his whole sentimental convention and, second, to

acceptance of the reality of this absurd little person and ultimately to delighted enlistment in the tension and truth of her maiden dilemma. He manages this, it seems to me, in a number of clear and legitimate ways: by setting her in a crux which, however much he chooses to cloy it, is inherently genuine and apposite to her way of life; by furnishing her with neatly counterpoised troops of friends and foes; by boning her fragility with an impressive willowy toughness and so making the balance reside in her own able little armory of innate powers, her craft and her ethics, her fanatical ability to cope—always a credible middle-class engine; by the pathos of the spectacle of the helpless old parents, quaking somewhere in the dim hinterland, hanging on with palpitations from letter to letter.

But still more interestingly Richardson satisfies our wish for satire and our sense of the motley truth of human personality by making Pamela, in little ways that can do her no basic harm, a figure of fun. The obvious traits in this line are her prolixity, her fondness for dull particularity, her transparent rationalizations (". . . he had this moment sent me five guineas, by Mrs. Jervis, as a present for my pocket; so I shall be very rich; for as *she* brought them, I thought I might take them"); her disingenuous vanity ("'Alas, Sir,' said I, my master coming up, 'mine is but a borrowed shine, like that of the moon. Here is the sun, to whose fervent glow of generosity I owe all the faint lustre that your goodness is pleased to look upon with so much kind distinction' "). And while equipping her with these harmless vices Richardson supplies her as well with considerable insight into them— that is, with self-knowledge. She knows that she is windy, and that it is part of her charm; she knows that she can be tiresomely circumstantial, that she is prone to construe motives to her own advantage, that she has a prehensile ear for praise. Our knowledge of her knowledge makes her immensely more tangible to our credence. Surely, for an allegorical figure, this is a creature strikingly rich; and, for one supposedly anemic, amusingly full of blood. Pamela must be the liveliest incarnation of chastity ever made. She is its abstract embodiment but she is also thoroughly concrete—fully clothed in bright and fluent particularity.

In further testimony to the realistic aspects of Richardson's characterization we should cite his handling of the brother-sister relationship between Mr. B. and Lady Davers. Considered singly, each is a type figure if not a purely allegorical one—though Lady Davers is a good deal more convincing as a human being than her brother. In spite of their individual stiffness, however, their behavior in their special office as siblings is perfectly life like and very vivid as Richardson manages them. Their interaction is colored by a complex ambiguity that is both affecting and comic, and is beautifully functional in the novel's plot tissue. I am thinking now mainly of the way in which the physical and emotional maturity of the two is conditioned and complicated by an interesting remnant childishness, by strong passions inherent, first, in the nature of each, but aggravated and set in violent motion by the multiplied facts of their past relationship together as children—their mingled recollection of past trauma and past felicity, the insight of each into his own foibles and those of his fellow, the impetuousness, stubbornness, and headlong arrogance which they wear like a family livery and which they recognize, fear, despise, and finally forgive in each other. All of this is enriched by the purest kind of fraternal affection and respect that is not sentimental at all, and all of it, it seems to me, is deeply imagined and finely done by Richardson; it is one of the best things in the book, and one of the truest.

Perhaps we can review most of the remaining virtues of Richardson's realism under the heading of solidity: here again I borrow a phrase from Henry James's classic essay, where "solidity of specification" is his parenthetical equivalent for "the air of reality"—which we remember was for James "the supreme virtue of a novel." By solidity James meant that effect of depth and thickness which enjoins belief, and he felt this effect was mainly to be achieved by fullness and aptness of circumstantial detail. Now whatever else *Pamela* has or has not, it has solidity. Its solidity is in important part a matter of simple accumulation and artful selection of detail—every incident, every shift of manner or motive, abundantly furnished with data for the five senses to convince us of its actuality by reason of its situation in time and space and specific environment. Of many possible illustrations of this we may note just a few. How real and how focal become those first four fatal guineas: "I send them by John our footman, who goes your way: but he does not know what he carries, because I seal them up in one of the little pill-boxes, which my lady had, wrapped close in paper, that they mayn't chink; and be sure don't open it before him." How additionally palpable and comic for his costume is the seducer from the closet: ". . . O dreadful! out rushed my master in a rich silk and silver morning gown." Consider the verisimilitude of a single detail as Pamela squeezes through the bars of her boudoir prison, ". . . not without some difficulty, sticking a little at my hips." How lively and vivid is the flashing vignette of those three relics of Mr. B.'s unregenerate youth when they come to call on him as stately Benedict: ". . . three mad rakes they seemed to be, setting up a hunting note, as soon as they came to the gate, that made the court-yard echo again: and smacking their whips in concert." Or consider the abundant factuality of those three enlightening catalogs, Mr. B.'s "naughty articles," as Pamela calls them, her recitative of her proposed regimen as country wife, and the forty-eight points of her gloss from her husband's "awful lecture."

[The remainder of the essay is devoted to a discussion of the moral issue and a defense of the novel against what Mr. Reid would contend is a further example of critical crudity and overemphasis. The difficulties of Pamela's position are reviewed, and the integrity of her defense of her chastity and the genuineness of her final love for Mr. B. and of her acceptance of him are argued, with the whole matter considered in the light of the moral climate of her age and class as Richardson conventionally and pragmatically posits it—ED.]

Richardson is not of the company of the "thought-divers," as Melville called them, the men with the "red eyes," that much is clear. But he is no joke, and I think it is time we stopped patronizing him. He is, as I have tried to argue, a shaggy amateur artist who should have been great, a man whose genius remained unfulfilled because it was unconscious. His originality is immense, and so, as everyone admits, is his historical service. . . . It is certainly true that Fielding had to reform the solid but simple-minded morality of *Pamela*. And it is true that Fielding and others had to teach the novel niceties of structure—selection and proportion—and grace and economy of movement; but aside from that there was little that anybody needed to teach Richardson, technically, about the writing of a novel. He knew how it was done, and he knew how to keep the anesthetic of Puritan morality from immobilizing life. That is the very considerable artistic achievement of this novel. We need not condescend to it, but read it.

Love and the Novel: *Pamela*

by Ian Watt

The importance of Richardson's position in the tradition of the novel was largely due to his success in dealing with several of the major formal problems which Defoe had left unsolved. The most important of them was probably that of plot, and here Richardson's solution was remarkably simple: he avoided an episodic plot by basing his novels on a single action, a courtship. It is no doubt odd that so fateful a literary revolution should have been brought about with so ancient a literary weapon; but—and this is the theme of the present chapter—in Richardson's hands it revealed new powers.

*　*　*

During Richardson's lifetime . . . many important and complex changes in the ways that the sexes oriented themselves to their roles* were already far advanced. These changes are of considerable intrinsic interest, since they herald the establishment of what is substantially the concept of courtship, marriage and the feminine role that has obtained most widely in the last two centuries. The reason for our interest in them here, however, is of a more directly literary nature: it derives from the fact that these social and psychological changes go far to explain two of the major qualities posed by *Pamela*: its formal unity, and its peculiar combination of moral purity and impurity.

Dr. Johnson, with the *novella* in mind, defined a "novel" as a "small tale, generally of love." When *Pamela* appeared it was called a "dilated novel," [1] because its subject was essentially the single amorous episode which previous short novels had usually been concerned with, but its treatment was on a scale much closer to that of a romance.

---

* [Matters discussed at length by Mr. Watt in the earlier sections of the chapter.]
[1] *Cit.* George Sherburn, "The Restoration and Eighteenth Century," *A Literary History of England,* ed. Baugh (New York, 1948), p. 803.

The direct connection between this change of scale and the tremendous importance which Richardson allotted to sexual morality is made clear by the contrast with Defoe. In Defoe's novels sexual encounters, marital or otherwise, are treated as minor episodes within the larger context of the pursuit of economic security. Moll Flanders is "tricked once by that cheat called love," [2] but it is a beginning, not an end; while Colonel Jacque comments on his faithful wife Moggy's "slip in her younger days" that "it was of small consequence to me one way or another." [3]

In the world of *Pamela* such off-handedness is inconceivable, for there, in the words of Henry Brooke,

> The woman no redemption knows
> The wounds of honour never close.[4]

Mr. B., of course, regards Pamela's acceptance of such a view as evidence that her "head is turned by romances and such idle stuff," but he is wrong. The ideal chastity of the romance heroines had been very completely incorporated into the general moral outlook; it was in much more humdrum literary sources that Pamela had "read that many a man has been ashamed of his wicked attempts, when he has been repulsed," and chanced "a night or two before" upon the crucial slogan which she announces in appropriate circumstances—"May I never survive, one moment, that fatal one in which I shall forfeit my innocence!" It was also, presumably, from some conduct book, although this time no literary indebtedness is acknowledged, that Pamela learned that "Millions of gold will not purchase one happy moment of reflection on a past mis-spent life." [5]

Defoe's heroines, of course, would not have thought twice, even for rewards much less than Mr. B.'s five hundred guineas: the novel is born because Pamela makes her epic resistance to a "fate worse than death," that significantly euphemistic hyperbole which loomed so large in the later history of fiction.

There is, of course, nothing inherently new in making a fictional heroine regard her chastity as a supreme value; what was new was that Richardson attributed such motives to a servant-girl: for whereas romance had usually exalted feminine chastity, the other forms of fiction which dealt with characters of humbler social origins had tended to take an opposite view of feminine psychology. It is this historical and literary perspective which makes clear the importance of *Pamela*: Richardson's novel represents the first complete confluence of two previously opposed traditions in fiction; it combines "high" and "low"

[2] *Moll Flanders,* ed. Aitken (London, 1902), I, 57.
[3] Ed. Aitken (London, 1902), II, 90.
[4] *Collection of Pieces,* 1778, II, 45.
[5] *Pamela,* Everyman Edition, I, 78, 31, 20, 169.

motives, and, even more important, it portrays the conflict between the two.

Richardson thus initiated the novel's radical departure from the *Stiltrennung* in the crucial area of sexual relations. Not only so: he also broke down the separation of "high" and "low life"—the class aspect of the *Stiltrennung,* and for the same reason. The movement for moral reform . . . tended to be mainly supported by the middle class, who fortified their outlook as a group with the assumption that their social superiors were their moral inferiors. This, of course, is the situation in *Pamela*—the rakish squire versus the humble but virtuous maid—and it lends the story a much larger significance than the purely individual matters at issue between the protagonists.

This use of the conflict between social classes is typical of the novel in general; its literary mode is radically particular, but it achieves a universality of meaning by making its individual actions and characters represent larger social issues. Defoe's plots are not such as to allow the relationships between his characters to go very far in developing this type of significance, whereas the much greater simplicity of the action of *Pamela* makes it far easier for the struggles of Pamela and Mr. B. to mirror larger contemporary conflicts between two classes and their way of life.

The enactment of the triumph of the middle-class code in sexual ethics brings with it, not only Mr. B.'s offer of marriage, but his complete re-education in the proper attitude to sex and marriage. These, of course, are mainly a matter of subjective personal values, and their adjustment involves a progressive revelation throughout the novel of the inner lives of the protagonists which continues until the hero's conversion is so complete that he becomes a "Puritan" [6] as far as Lady Davers is concerned.

The relationship between Pamela and Mr. B. is therefore able to develop a much richer psychological and moral content than that between the traditional lovers in romance. The barriers between them that have to be broken down are not external and contrived but internal and real; and for this reason, combined with the fact that these barriers are based on the differences in their respective class outlooks, the dialogue between the lovers is not, as it is in romance, a conventional exercise in rhetoric, but an exploration of the forces that have made them what they are.

There is one final and very important contribution to the structure of *Pamela* which is directly related both to the middle-class Puritan sexual code, and to the major difference between that code and the tradition of courtly love.

Courtly love separated the sexual roles in a similar way—the carnal male adored the godlike purity of the female, and the contradiction between the two roles was absolute. In theory, at least; for if the lady yielded to her lover's suit it meant a total breakdown of the convention. Puritanism, however, by providing marriage with a large spiritual and social meaning, provided a possible bridge between the spirit and the flesh, between the convention and social reality. The bridge was not an easy one, because, as Richardson had explained in his popular contribution to the *Rambler* in 1751, the feminine role in courtship made it immoral as well as impolitic for a girl to allow herself to feel love for a suitor until he had actually asked for her hand in marriage.[7] The very difficulty, however, and the sudden reversal of the lady's attitude which was implied, supplied Richardson with a vital plot resource, since it made it possible for Richardson to withhold from us any idea of Pamela's real feelings towards Mr. B. until the crisis in the action.

When Pamela leaves him to return to her parents it appears certain that all is over between them; actually a counter-movement at once begins. On the one hand, she is surprised to discover "something so strange . . . so *unexpected*" in her feelings that she is forced to wonder whether she is not in fact sorry to be leaving;[8] on the other hand, Mr. B.'s deepest feelings, as revealed in his parting letter, show that he is not merely the stereotype of the licentious squire but a man whose intentions may become honest, and who may quite possibly be a fit mate for Pamela. These sudden revelations of the disparity between the conventional and the actual attitudes of the lovers thus enabled Richardson to work out their relationship in a plot of the type which Aristotle considered to be the best, a complex action in which the peripety and the recognition coincide. The dramatic resolution of the plot of *Pamela*, in fact, was made possible by the actual moral and social attitudes of the time, which had produced an unprecedented disparity between the conventional roles of the sexes and the actual tenor of the oracles of the heart.

This conflict between public and private attitudes is one with which the novel in general has been much concerned, and which it is indeed peculiarly fitted to portray. There is, however, considerable doubt as to how far Richardson was aware of the duplicities involved in the feminine role, or as to how we should interpret the narrative which embodies them.

As is well known, *Pamela* has always been subject to very contradictory interpretations. Soon after its first publication one anonymous pamphleteer reported that there were, "particularly among the

---

[7] No. 97. It was the most popular of the *Ramblers*, according to Walter Graham (*English Literary Periodicals*, New York, 1930, p. 120).

[8] I, 222.

ladies, two different parties, *Pamelists* and *Antipamelists,"* who dis-
agreed as to "whether the young virgin was an example for ladies to
follow . . . or . . . a hypocritical crafty girl . . . who understands
the art of bringing a man to her lure." [9] The most famous work in the
controversy, of course, is *Shamela*, where, as his title implies, Fielding
interpreted Richardson's heroine as a hypocrite whose masterly de-
ployment of the resources of the feminine role enabled her to entrap
a rich booby into marriage, although her purity did not in fact go
beyond the conventional public pretence suggested by Mrs. Lucretia
Jarvis when she speaks of the need to avoid "what we women call
rude, when done in the presence of others." [10]

Fielding's pamphlet certainly draws attention to an important
ambiguity in *Pamela*, but when later critics suggest that we must
choose between Fielding's interpretation or Richardson's they are
surely overlooking the possibility that the ambiguity need not spring
from conscious duplicity on Pamela's part, since it is implicit in the
feminine code by which she acts. It seems evident, for example, that
the code's tremendous emphasis on the differentiation of the sexes in
behaviour and dress is open to a very similar criticism to that which
Fielding made of *Pamela*. "Decency," as Bernard Shaw has reminded
us, "is indecency's conspiracy of silence," and the concern of the
eighteenth-century moralists with feminine purity suggests imagina-
tions only too ready to colour everything with impure sexual signifi-
cances.

Sarah Fielding speaks in *Ophelia* (1760) of how Mrs. Darkins thought
a "girl ought not to set eyes on a baby that was not of the feminine
gender"; [11] the corrupt assumptions of this attitude are made clear
when we remember that it is the lecherous Lady Wishfort in Con-
greve's *Way of the World* who prided herself on not allowing her
infant daughter to play with little boys.[12] Similarly, we can interpret
Addison's campaign against naked bosoms in the *Guardian*,[13] by recalling that Tartuffe's unhealthy prurience is revealed by his throwing
a handkerchief over Dorine's breasts,[14] and Bridget Allworthy's by her
scandalised outcry against the revelatory Sunday finery of the farmers'
daughters.[15] Richardson's own mind was certainly obsessed with sex
in a similar way, as we can see in some of his own pronouncements on
sexual modesty. In the *Familiar Letters*, for example, writing in the
guise of an uncle, he chides his niece's "manly air" in these terms: "I

[9] *The Tablet, or Picture of Real Life,* 1762, p. 14.
[10] Letter VII.
[11] II, 42.
[12] Act V, sc. v.
[13] No. 116 (1713).
[14] *Tartuffe,* Act III, sc. ii.
[15] *Tom Jones,* Bk. I, ch. 8.

have been particularly offended . . . at your *new riding-habit*; which is made so extravagantly in the mode, that one cannot easily distinguish your sex by it. For you look neither like a *modest girl* in it, nor an *agreeable boy*." [16]

The ambivalent implications of a conspicuous concern for feminine modesty suggest themselves with equal force in the case of Richardson's heroine. It is certainly tempting to explain her continual concern with decency of dress, for example, by reference to the views of Dr. Gregory, an influential exponent of the new feminine code: in his *Father's Legacy to His Daughters* (1774) he concluded his warnings against "denudation" with the Machiavellian parenthesis—"The finest bosom in nature is not so fine as what imagination forms." [17] Be that as it may, there is at least no doubt that Mr. B. finds Pamela's virtuous resistance infinitely more provocative than any compliance could have been, and thus provides an involuntary tribute to the efficacy of the new feminine role in encompassing its ultimate aim.

That, however, does not justify us in assuming, as the Fielding interpretation suggests, that Pamela is only modest because she wants to entrap Mr. B. It is surely better to regard her as a real person whose actions are the result of the complexities of her situation and of the effects, both conscious and unconscious, of the feminine code. Steele pointed out that prude and coquette are alike in that they have "the distinction of sex in all their thoughts, words and actions": [18] the code that commanded the allegiance of Pamela and her author is itself open to either interpretation. Similarly, although Pamela's acceptance of Mr. B. as a husband suggests that she regards his early advances as less heinous than she could publicly admit at the time, the inconsistency can be fully explained as the result of the falsity of the public code, rather than of her own character. Certainly if we condemn Pamela for such departures from absolute openness and sincerity in courtship, we must not forget how widely the charge could be brought against others in similar circumstances, both in her age and in ours.

Richardson's own attitude is difficult to determine. Like his heroine, he is alternately fascinated and repelled by Mr. B.'s licentious attempts, and his moral protestations are not wholly convincing. As an artist, however, Richardson seems to have been more aware of both points of view with respect to Pamela's sexual ethics than has been generally recognised, although he implicitly disavows the opposite position by making the odious Mrs. Jewkes its most vocal representative. When Pamela, for example, remarks that "to rob a person of her virtue is

---

[16] Letter 90.
[17] 1822 ed., p. 47.
[18] *Cit.* R. P. Utter and G. B. Needham, *Pamela's Daughters* (London, 1937), p. 64.

worse than cutting her throat" she answers with an incomprehension
which, though lamentable, is not without illustrious precedent: "Why
now, how strangely you talk! Are not the two sexes made for one another? Is it not natural for a gentleman to love a pretty woman? And
suppose he can obtain his desires, is that so bad as cutting her throat?"
The remark would not be out of place in *Shamela*; nor would Mrs.
Jewkes's contemptuous retort when Pamela begs her not to let the
master in lest she be undone—"Mighty piece of undone!" [19]

As a novelist, then, Richardson is capable of considerable objectivity;
but it is clear that as a conscious moralist he is completely on the side
of Pamela, and it is here that the most serious objections to his novel
arise. His sub-title, "Virtue Rewarded," draws attention to the im-
mitigable vulgarity of the book's moral texture; it is surely evident
that Pamela is in any case chaste only in a very technical sense which
is of scant interest to the morally perceptive, and that Fielding hit
upon the major moral defect of the story when he made Shamela remark: "I thought once of making a little fortune by my person. I now
intend to make a great one by my virtue." [20] As to Mr. B.'s vaunted
reformation it is difficult to see that it amounts to any more than a
promise, in Mandeville's words, "never to be a deer-stealer, upon condition that he shall have venison of his own." [21]

Mandeville, of course, was the self-appointed *agent provocateur* of
the bourgeois unconscious, determined to draw attention to all the
perplexities in public morality which Addison and Richardson were
determined to ignore; and his cynical analogy brings us back to the
very considerable extent to which the problems raised by Richardson's
treatment of marriage are typical of modern Western culture as a
whole. If we . . . [compare] *Pamela* with Chaucer's *Troilus and
Criseyde* or Shakespeare's *Romeo and Juliet* it is surely apparent that
although Richardson is much purer in his language and his overt
attitudes, his work nevertheless concentrates much more exclusively on
the sexual relationship itself. This combination has had a very wide
currency in fiction since then and has even spread to the cinema. In
the Hollywood film, as in the type of popular fiction which Richardson initiated, we have an unprecedentedly drastic and detailed Puritan
censorship in conjunction with a form of art which is historically
unique in its concentration on arousing sexual interests: while in it
marriage figures as the moral *deus ex machina* which, as James
Fordyce said of marriage in comedy, "is converted into a sponge, to
wipe out in a single stroke the stain of guilt." [22]

The cause of this duality—in Richardson's time as in ours—is
presumably that the tabooed object is always an indication of the

[19] *Pamela*, I, 95–96, 174.
[20] *Shamela*, Letter 10.
[21] *Fable of the Bees*, I, 161.
[22] *Sermons to Young Women*, 1766, I, 156.

deepest interest of the society that forbids. All the forces that combined to intensify the prohibitions against sexual activity outside marriage, tended in practice to increase the importance of sex in the total
picture of human life. That they did so in Richardson was suggested by
one of his contemporary critics, the anonymous "Lover of Virtue" who
produced some *Critical Remarks on Sir Charles Grandison, Clarissa
and Pamela* (1754). He coupled the fact that "Love, eternal Love, is
the subject, the burthen of all your writings" with Richardson's
tremendous accentuation of what he called the "political chastity"
about which "you and your heroines make such a rout and a pother,"
a chastity which in his opinion compared very unfavourably with that
of the women of ancient Greece. Even so, the writer was at a loss to
understand why so many "public-spirited penmen" thought it necessary to employ "all their art and eloquence to keep people in re-
membrance, that they were composed of different sexes" when "provident nature" unassisted could be trusted to "prevent the world from
coming to an end." [23] The explanation, of course, was that the repres-
sion of the instincts of "provident nature," combined with the increasing concealment of what our culture, with eloquent indirection,
calls "the facts of life," produced needs in the public which had to be
gratified. One of the main functions of the novel since Richardson, it
may be suggested, has been to serve a fictional initiation rite into the
most fundamental mystery of its society.

Only by some such hypothesis can we explain the later course of the
novel, or the remarkable paradox that Richardson, a leader in the
crusade for sexual reform, and an avowed enemy of love both in its
romantic and fleshly aspects,** should have signalised his entry into
the history of literature by a work which gave a more detailed account
of a single amorous intrigue than had ever been produced before. It
would seem that the opposite qualities in Richardson's outlook, his
Puritanism and his prurience, are the result of the same forces, and
this no doubt explains why their effects are so intricately connected.
The complexities of the forces juxtaposed are largely responsible for
the unique literary qualities which *Pamela* brought into fiction: they
make possible a detailed presentation of a personal relationship enriched by a series of developing contrasts between the ideal and the
real, the apparent and the actual, the spiritual and the physical, the
conscious and the unconscious. But if the latent ambiguities of the
sexual code helped Richardson to produce the first true novel, they
at the same time conspired to create something that was new and
prophetic in quite another sense: a work that could be praised from
the pulpit and yet attacked as pornography, a work that gratified the
reading public with the combined attractions of a sermon and a striptease.

[23] Pp. 38, 35, 27–30, 39.
** [Discussed in the earlier sections of the chapter.]

Pamela

by R. F. Brissenden

There has perhaps never been a literary success quite like that of
Pamela. Certainly no previous work of fiction had ever attained such
rapid, widespread and enduring popularity, and few have since.
Pamela seems to have appealed to every sort of potential reader, and
although judged by modern standards the reading public at this time
formed only a small proportion of the general population the book
enjoyed a wide circulation. Fashionable ladies smiled at the heroine's
"lowness," but wept in their chambers over her trials; her virtue was
praised in the pulpit; and, according to one story, the villagers at
Slough rang the church bells to celebrate her marriage. Within a year
Pamela had run through six impressions and had been translated into
French. Translations into other languages soon followed; and it eventually became more popular on the Continent, where it inspired not
only other novels but also several plays and an opera, than in England.
Pamela became the archetypal Cinderella story of the age—in Lady
Mary Wortley Montagu's phrase, "the joy of the chambermaids of all
nations." Probably no other novel was read by so many people in the
eighteenth century: in the general imagination of the period Pamela
herself acquired something of the status of a mythical figure.

How are we to account for the extraordinary popularity of this
novel? Part of the answer lies simply in its quality as a work of fiction:
although the book as a whole may be justly criticized for its uneven-
ness, its crudity, and its sentimentality, the first portion of the novel,
that dealing with Mr. B.'s various attempts to seduce Pamela, is a lively
and convincing piece of writing. Moreover the situation is presented
with a psychological realism and a moral seriousness which were almost completely new in English fiction. These things would not have
been enough in themselves, however: what guaranteed the success of
Pamela was that in so many respects it was the right book at the right
time. Since the end of the seventeenth century the demand for fiction
had been growing steadily, largely as a result of an increase in the

"Pamela" *by R. F. Brissenden. From* Samuel Richardson *(London: Longmans,
Green and Co., Ltd. for the British Council and the National Book League, 1958),
pp. 12–21. Copyright © 1958 by R. F. Brissenden. Reprinted by permission of the
author and the British Council.*

number of middle-class people, especially women, with enough leisure for reading. "The world is so taken up of late with novels and romances, that it will be hard for a private history to be taken for genuine," complained Defoe in 1722 in his preface to *Moll Flanders*; and in 1740, the year in which Pamela was published, there were enough works of fiction in print and enough people wanting to read them for the first circulating library in London to be opened. But mere quantity was not enough to satisfy this developing appetite: the majority of the "novels and romances" published at this time were, as Richardson states on the title page of *Pamela*, "Pieces calculated for Amusement only." Whether they tended also to "inflame the Minds they should instruct" is doubtful. Though their plots and titles are often erotic enough, the stories themselves are for the most part shallow, insipid and incredible. When something realistic, like Defoe's brilliant documentary narratives of contemporary life, was produced, it lacked psychological depth and subtlety.

Moreover, people wanted to be instructed as well as amused: it was their gentle didacticism as much as anything else which made *The Tatler* and *The Spectator* so popular; and even in this increasingly secular age books on religious subjects still constituted the largest single category of those published each year. Allegories like *The Pilgrim's Progress*, works of practical piety, such as *The Whole Duty of Man*, *Holy Living and Holy Dying*, and Defoe's various *Family Instructors* went through dozens of editions, and collections of sermons were best sellers. And the practicality of these and innumerable similar works was often as important as their piety: they were concerned with the most pressing social problems of the day—the status of women, the rearing of children, the extent to which private convictions should be allowed to conflict with social responsibilities. The author of *The Whole Duty of Man* spends more space discussing man's duty to his neighbours than in discussing his duty to God; and Defoe, in the dramatic dialogues in *Religious Courtship* is more concerned with problems of marriage than with problems of religion.

This is the tradition in which *Pamela*, like the *Familiar Letters*, was initially conceived. When Richardson began to write *Pamela* he probably had no intention of producing a novel at all. As the subtitle, *Virtue Rewarded*, indicates, his purpose was simply to use his story to demonstrate both that servant girls ought to resist the amorous advances of their masters and that Providence will look after them if they do. But in spite of his modest aim the conduct-book parable came alive in his hands and developed into a novel.

Richardson became a novelist primarily because he had the novelist's genius. But this genius needed something to release it. For Richardson this was effected through his intense concern with certain moral issues, a concern which was the result of a profound conflict within his own personality, a conflict between a strong and sympathetic sense of justice and an innate and almost pathological timidity. This conflict is reflected in all his writings: indeed it is out of the attempt to resolve it that his novels are born.

In the Preface to the *Familiar Letters* Richardson, speaking of himself in the third person, states that it has been his purpose through the letters

> to inculcate the Principles of *Virtue* and *Benevolence;* to describe *properly* and recommend *strongly,* the SOCIAL and RELATIVE DUTIES. . . .
> Particularly, he has endeavoured to point out the Duty of a *Servant* not a *Slave;* the Duty of a *Master* not a *Tyrant;* that of a *Parent,* not as a Person morose and sour, and hard to be pleased; but mild, indulgent, kind, and such a one as would rather govern by *Persuasion* than *Force.*

This could serve as an introduction to everything he ever wrote. The "SOCIAL and RELATIVE DUTIES" are, in some form or other the theme of all his novels. He is preoccupied by the problem of the relation between the individual and the various social groups to which he belongs. What are the obligations which we owe to those who are socially either our superiors or our inferiors? What are the obligations which, in common humanity, we owe to others irrespective of class, sex, creed or nationality? And what are we to do when these two sets of duties come into conflict? Stated in the most general terms, these are the questions which Richardson continually raises and seeks to answer in his novels.

In some form or other these are the questions with which all serious novelists are concerned. Richardson is particularly interesting, however, because to begin with his attitude to these matters was not that of a novelist at all: he approached the whole problem of human conduct as a moral propagandist rather than an artist. But through the attempt to apply his dogmatic and relatively simple moral theory to the practical and untidy realities of life he developed, by a process of forced and often painful growth, not only into a novelist but also into a moral and social thinker of some force and profundity.

The process can be observed very clearly in *Pamela.* At the superficial level it is a tract on the virtues of chastity and, more particularly, dutifulness. The heroine succeeds in getting Mr. B. to marry her because no matter how sadistically he tries her she endeavours to treat him still with the respect to which as her master and as a man he is "properly" entitled. The hypocritical twists and subterfuges through which Pamela goes—or is forced to go by Richardson—in order to keep up this façade of respect are amongst the more unpleasant and ridiculous features of the novel; and if Pamela's dutifulness were the only explanation for the eventual marriage of the hero and heroine

the book would have been forgotten long ago. But the situation is
more complex than it seems at first: Pamela finally gets her man not
because she is dutiful to him, but because she succeeds in convincing
him that he owes a duty to her, not merely as a woman but simply as
a human being. She does this by distinguishing with scrupulous
thoroughness between the occasions on which he deserves to be re-
spected and those on which he forfeits this right by trying to demand
her obedience in an "improper" way. After his attempt on her virtue
in the summerhouse, for instance, Pamela announces rebelliously that
she won't stay:

> You won't, hussy! said he: Do you know whom you speak to? I lost
> all fear and all respect, and said, Yes, I do, Sir, too well!—well may
> I forget that I am your servant, when you forget what belongs to a
> master.

The scene is typical: every encounter between the two follows the same
pattern of angry, passionate and frustrated argument. So long as the
debate is verbal Pamela always wins; and despite Mr. B.'s attempts to
gain her affection by kidnapping and imprisoning her she gradually
achieves more and more real freedom. Whenever her exasperated master descends to more direct methods she is always saved by her "happy
knack at falling into fits."

But the book is much more than a debate about the rights of
women. Although Mr. B.'s wooing of his beautiful servant girl is conducted in terms of rights and duties, it is infused with powerful feeling.
Whenever the two lovers come into each other's presence the emotional temperature rises immediately. There is little affection between
them—their meetings almost always end in impotent fury on one side
and tears on the other—but their attraction for each other, distorted
and frustrated though it may be, is undoubtedly there. In this first
novel there is considerable crudeness and naïvety in Richardson's
presentation of sexual passion; and his characterization of Mr. B. can
scarcely be called successful: as one contemporary critic remarked
rather dryly, it is just as well that the author has informed us that
Mr. B. "had been a great rake, and had debauch'd several women
. . . for from his whole behaviour towards his Pamela, one should be
apt to think him the meerest novice in the world." But despite the
gaucheries both of Mr. B., and of Richardson himself, one cannot
deny the strength and complexity of feeling which develops as the
novel unfolds. Psychological realism such as this, though common
enough in drama, was something new in English fiction, and it had
an immediate appeal to the contemporary reading public. Even today
the first section of *Pamela,* that in which the story of the courtship is
told, can hold and excite the interest. Once the marriage has occurred,

however, the tension disappears, and apart from one or two scenes the
rest of the book, in which the preacher is allowed to take over almost
completely from the novelist, is dull, worthless stuff.

Much of the power in the first part of *Pamela* arises from that sup-
pressed and morbid sexual passion which burns like a slow fire
beneath the surface of all this writer's work. But an equally important
element in the complex of feelings which both inspired and were re-
leased by the writing of this and the other novels is Richardson's
obsession with the moral and social problems of the rights of the individual. The two sets of feelings are, in fact, inextricably involved;
the sexual conflict in his novels always reflects a social struggle of
much wider significance. Pamela and Mr. B., like all Richardson's
lovers, express their "love" for each other in debates about rights and
duties; and in one way the battle in which they are all involved is not
sexual at all. Richardson's heroines are all democrats: their most
fundamental desire is that their suitors should "respect" them; that is,
should accord them their rights as individual human beings before
beginning to treat them as women. As Pamela says to Mr. B.,

> Whatever you have to propose, whatever you intend by me, let my
> assent be that of a free person, mean as I am, and not of a sordid slave,
> who is to be threatened and frightened into a compliance.

In a sense this is a denial of sex; and the way in which Pamela and
Clarissa argue with their lovers and use tears and fits in an attempt to
escape from the physical realities of the sexual situation is undoubtedly
"sentimental." But from another point of view there is nothing sentimental at all in their attitude: Richardson's heroines have no illusions
about the disadvantages of belonging to the weaker sex. As Anne
Howe, who represents the voice of common sense in *Clarissa*, remarks,
there is nothing very glorious in being "cajoled, wire-drawn and
ensnared, like silly birds into a state of bondage . . . courted as
princesses for a few weeks, in order to be treated as slaves for the rest
of our lives." In a society dominated by men such ideas, especially
when they are held by a mere maidservant as Pamela was, are socially
rather embarrassing; and there can be no doubt that much of the
ridicule which Richardson's first novel attracted, was aroused by the
brilliant insubordination of his heroine. Parody is, more often than
not, just as much an attempt to laugh an uncomfortable truth out of
existence as it is to ridicule error, hypocrisy and dullness. *Shamela*'s
most obvious target is the genuine sentimentality and hypocrisy of
Richardson; but Fielding also wrote it in the effort to make Pamela
conform, to force her into the more easily acceptable mould of the
feminine fortune hunter. But Pamela is far too complicated to be
forced into any pattern. Indeed it is because she refuses to fit into the

usual pattern, refuses to behave like Moll Flanders or Roxana, that she becomes the first real heroine in English fiction.

Pamela's complexity reflects the complexity of Richardson himself. As Brian Downs has so aptly put it, he wrote from "a divided heart." And the divisions, the inner conflicts in Richardson's heart, are significant not simply because they provided the impetus for writing the novels, and generated the complex feeling with which they are charged, but also because they symbolized in a personal and dramatic form some of the most fundamental problems of the society in which he lived. Richardson's guilts and fears were the guilts and fears of his age; and when he turned his unwitting eyes in upon the dark corners of his own soul his readers felt that theirs were being exposed too. "C'est lui," wrote Diderot, "qui porte le flambeau au fond de la caverne."

Richardson was not a happy man. Craving affection he had learnt to mistrust it, and instead to pin all his hopes of emotional security on the exercise of power. "There can be no love without fear!" he maintained: children must learn to respect their parents, and wives their husbands, before they can love them. Timid, lonely and socially diffident, he drew great satisfaction from the influence and respect which his position as a paterfamilias, a successful printer, and later a successful novelist brought him. Clearly he had a vested interest in trying to preserve those conventions of the social order in which his own small authority rested. Yet he was blessed (or cursed) with that primary innocence and honesty of vision which all great artists possess. If suffering or injustice existed he could not blind himself to them, nor, in the last resort, forgive himself for them, even when the suffering and injustice were the direct result of those aspects of the social structure which it was plainly in his own interest to leave undisturbed. Indeed these were the things which seemed to fascinate him most: although in real life he enjoyed exercising his rights as a man, a husband, a father and a bourgeois snob, in his novels he subjected the question of the validity of these rights to a most painful and searching examination.

His attitude to women, to children and to the family was essentially ambivalent: a compound of sympathy and hatred, arrogance and fear, pride and guilt. His sympathy for women, for instance, made him a passionate advocate of their rights; but at the same time his outraged and terrified male ego, in the nightmare figures of Mr. B., Lovelace, and the kind but implacable Grandison, ensured that the Pamelas and Clarissas of this world should be punished for their rebelliousness, and the Charlotte Grandisons and Harriet Byrons kept firmly in their place.

It seems clear that when Richardson began to write *Pamela* he had

no great understanding or control of the conflicting inner forces he
was about to release. In a very real sense he did not know what he was
doing: almost without his realizing it his simple moral tract somehow
turned into a novel. In the process he discovered his powers—but he
did not discover how to organize and discipline them. Because of this
the characterization and structure of his first novel are twisted out of
shape, and the book as a whole displays most bewildering contradic-
tions in tone and intention. But in the successful sections of the novel
his ability, the promise of his genius, is clearly manifest. The source
is obvious too: the most vital element in the book, the thing that
made it so spectacularly successful in its own day, is its confused but
angry concern with social injustice. And it is this rather than its
psychological realism that makes it still readable: Pamela's arguments
with Mr. B. are as lively and convincing today as when they were first
written. But the most impressive scene in *Pamela* is one in which Mr.
B. does not appear; it is the quarrel between Pamela and Mr. B.'s
sister, Lady Davers. By an almost theatrical, but no doubt unconscious,
contrivance Richardson is able in this scene to forget all those conventional notions of duty and decorum which lay a film of sentimentality and hypocrisy over so much of the novel. Lady Davers not only
does not know that Pamela is her brother's wife, but she is completely
unprepared to believe it. Pamela, however, knowing that she is indeed
married, and therefore Lady Davers' social equal, is perfectly sure of
her own position. Each of them is thus able to speak her mind with
perfect honesty, without false condescension on the one hand or false
humility on the other. The situation is electric: the dialogue, rapid
and colloquial, crackles back and forth—Pamela's dignified but
spirited defence of herself contrasting vividly with the passionate and
spiteful raging of Lady Davers. It is an ugly and perhaps slightly
hysterical scene, but it is savagely revealing. Its sheer dramatic power
is undeniable: it is the most sustained piece of writing in *Pamela*, and
one of the least cluttered or involved. Richardson's literary genius
here breaks free completely from the restrictive patterns of puritan
didactic literature; and it is patent that, given the right material and
the right opportunities to develop it, he should be able to produce a
work of fiction of considerable force and stature. In *Clarissa* this is
what he does: and if the title means anything, it is *Clarissa*, rather
than *Pamela* or *Joseph Andrews,* which should be called the first
English novel.

An Introduction to *Pamela*

by M. Kinkead-Weekes

In our own time the Antipamelists seem to have won the day, *Shamela* is vindicated, and there is widespread agreement that Pamela's conduct is hypocritical, whether consciously so or not. Indeed, critics are less concerned to proclaim this now than to point to the psychological realism of Richardson's creation, and to seek the source of both this and the moral confusion in his unquestioning identification with his heroine. By tapping her author's unconscious, on this view, *Pamela* reveals to us not only Richardson's confusions, but a typical and significant ambivalence in the whole Puritan ethos. As Steele pointed out, prude and coquette are alike in that they have "the distinction of sex in all their thoughts, words and actions"—this is why Pamela can seem to be either. The more indeed the moralist and his heroine proclaim their rejection of sexuality, the more they can be seen to be obsessed by it. We may also recall Mrs. Peachum's observation that "by keeping men off, you keep them on."

Yet only four years later Richardson completed *Clarissa*, about whose power and moral stature there is no less widespread agreement; and while there is much evidence of technical development, the moral and spiritual concerns of the two novels are remarkably similar. There is certainly no evidence of re-thinking deep enough to account for the radical discrepancy the critics discover between them. Disturbing, too, is the assumption that Richardson was an unconscious artist with little idea what he was doing, when it is coupled with a failure to examine the implications and complications of the new form he invented. For although Richardson wrote no formal essay on his art, he did scatter through his published and unpublished letters a large number of statements which show a surprisingly acute understanding of his problems.

What he invented was the dramatic novel, not merely the idea of writing in letters. The epistolary form is a means, not an end. It is an attempt to gain something of the immediacy of a playgoer's experi-

Introduction *by M. Kinkead-Weekes to the Everyman's Library Edition of Samuel Richardson's* Pamela, *pp. vi–xiii. Copyright,* ©, *1962 by J. M. Dent & Sons, Ltd. Reprinted by permission of E. P. Dutton & Co., Inc.*

ence; of getting to know characters directly, not through a narrative filter, and of watching an action unfold now, while one looks and listens. Richardson called his invention "writing to the moment." As often as he could he made his characters write during the crises of their affairs. Where this was impossible they write immediately afterwards; either in letters largely composed of dialogue and description of action and gesture, to convey the effect of watching a dramatic scene; or in letters of immediate self-analysis like extensions of dramatic soliloquy. Because these are written "to the moment" and not collectedly later, consciousness can be caught on the wing, and one can discover things about the characters that they do not yet know themselves.

Drama, moreover, is not merely a technique of writing. It is a kind of imaginative vision that is quite different from other kinds. In narrative the author tells you directly in his own words what he has conceived. In drama he has to see and communicate indirectly, by projecting his imagination into characters who reveal themselves without his mediation. The author himself is not there at all—he has become all his characters. Some are obviously closer to him than others, but we can only establish his own views when we understand the whole meaning that results from the conflicts he has created. The moment we identify him with one character, we begin to blind ourselves to that meaning.

Since we are given no direct guidance, it is more than ever important that we become alive to the full implications of the conflicts; that we enter the "points of view" of all the characters; and that we build up a much fuller understanding than any of them possesses. Indirect forms are much more difficult than direct ones, and demand closer, more subtle and sensitive reading. This is particularly so with Richardson because his moral world is one in which the minutiae of speech, dress and behaviour may be important revelations of the state of the heart and mind that prompts them. We have also to be sensitive to the implications of different styles, for "styles differ, too, as much as faces, and are indicative, generally beyond the power of disguise, of the mind of the writer."

We should also be very wary of treating dramatic characters as though they were real people. It is ironic that the more successful a dramatist is in putting one directly inside the minds of his characters the greater becomes the danger of distortion through analysing them as one would an acquaintance. For we tend to forget how crucially our knowledge is limited by and dependent on the method and form of the work of art. It may be unjustified to see incurable vanity in Pamela's continual repetition of the praise she receives; or evidence that her delicacy about sex is hypocritical when she details the attempts made on her, or passes on dubious jokes; or morbid introspection in her prolonged and brooding self-analysis. For these are all *formal* matters. There are several dramatic points of view, but only one of them "writes" the novel; so Pamela has to tell us all there is to tell and carry the whole burden of analysis. We on the other hand ought to distinguish what is genuinely self-revelatory from what is narrative or analytic, and know when psychological inferences are appropriate and when they are not. We may point to the formal crudity which creates such difficulties, but this is quite a different criticism. (It is here that Richardson's great formal development, the multiplication of foci in *Clarissa*, itself removes many of what had appeared to be moral objections to *Pamela*.) Again, our knowledge of characters must be controlled by the development of a novel's formal patterning, the artful relationship between its scenes. However artless Richardson may look, his scenes are carefully related, often in cycles each of which reorchestrates its predecessor. So the gift of clothes on which the novel opens is related to the important "clothes scene" of Letter XXIV. This in turn is parodied by B. in Letter XXVII, redeveloped in the "bundle scene" of Letter XXIX, given a new symbolic twist in Pamela's garments floating on the pond, another reorchestration on page 270, and a final pointing on page 449. Examples could be multiplied, but in all the psychological speculation about Pamela and her creator the meaning of this patterning has played no part.

Most important of all, the fact that the dramatic "kind" is the most exploratory type of novel has not been understood. As well as formal crudities there are several crudities of attitude and value in *Pamela*. Yet what is really significant is not that these exist, but that in so many cases Richardson is able, in developing his novel, to feel his way towards far deeper and finer values which he carried over and extended in *Clarissa*. While we identify him with his heroine, and pay no attention to the structural and textural development of his work, we shall fail to see that its significance and its achievement lie precisely in its *criticism* of the mental and moral world of the little girl of fifteen we meet at the beginning, even if—as may be the case—that world was Richardson's when he began to write. For a dramatic writer not only has to become several very different points of view; he also is forced to imagine how these look to one another, and has to try to resolve the conflicts that arise. Whatever values he may have held are likely to go through what Blake called the fire of thesis and antithesis; they are tested, realized, criticized—and they change.

The novel's first movement, up to the abduction of Pamela, is concerned with the day-to-day fluctuations of her struggle with her master. In this first conflict Richardson obviously uses her values to expose the implications of B.'s amoral world of pride and power; but in the process he discovers dangerous weaknesses in Pamela too. Hypocrisy is not one of them. Richardson saw the possibility of such a charge perfectly clearly—it is actually made by B. in Letter XXIV. But to Richardson this could only spring from a failure to understand how diametrically opposed to the world of the sex war with its laws of attraction and seduction the behaviour of Pamela is, as soon as one grasps what her new clothes symbolize. In that letter B.'s moral sensibility begins to be awakened. We have to be alive to the implications of what B. says and does to realize what is happening, but when we do the charge of hypocrisy is effectively refuted. What Richardson does discover about his heroine are the dangers that lie in her innate suspiciousness, which blinds her to the complex realities of other people; in her calculating prudence; and in her vanity and her inability to achieve real humility, social, moral or spiritual.

In the second movement Pamela is imprisoned. This is a period of "persecutions, oppressions and distress," but it is also a period of spiritual growth. It lasts, pointedly, for forty days and forty nights, and the presence of biblical language in the prayer which opens it, and in the scene by the pond at its heart, should indicate that the new conflict within Pamela herself has a religious dimension. Her greatest temptation in the wilderness has indeed nothing to do with B. Behind all her faults there lies a stubborn pride and self-reliance, and to be like this, for Richardson, is to court despair when one's human fallibility is inevitably exposed. Pamela's battles against despair, her struggles to regain true faith not only in God but in Man, lie at the very centre of the novel's meaning. At the first scene by the pond she discovers in her temptation to suicide the core of a new self-knowledge and humility. "And how do I know, but that God, who sees all the lurking vileness of my heart, may have permitted these sufferings on that very score, and to make me rely solely on his grace and assistance, who, perhaps, have too much prided myself in a vain dependence on my own foolish contrivances." In the carefully related second pond scene she adds faith in Man to faith in God, even though this means acting imprudently. For the first time she and her persecutor really meet and communicate as human beings.

Pamela's suspicion and timidity are not overcome in a day, but her happiness will depend on her ability to continue in her new-won faith. At first she fails disastrously. Her fear of a mock marriage makes her reject a genuine proposal from B., and at last she is given what she has constantly begged for, and is angrily dismissed to her parents. Now, however, she discovers (what the competent reader should have known from innumerable hints long before) the depth of her feeling for her persecutor. When he begs her to return, against all the dictates of pride and prudence, she does so in love and faith and makes her happiness and his regeneration possible.

Apart from the angry scenes with Lady Davers and the discovery of B.'s illegitimate daughter, the drama ends here. The rest of the

novel consists mainly of social visiting, in which the happy pair discuss
their history in public while Pamela is deluged with choric praise and
blessing; and of long discussions of the duties and proper behaviour
of man and wife—or, rather, largely of wife. The spinning out of the
novel is further evidence that Richardson was not primarily interested
in pursuit and capture, but one can see why readers find it tedious.
Yet it was important, for Richardson, to demonstrate the consistency
and integrity of Pamela's behaviour before and after her marriage;
and also to enforce the validity of her values over a wider field than
her struggles with B. could provide. The novel becomes a "Whole
Duty of Woman"; a fictional counterpart to the *Whole Duty of Man*
which Pamela sends to Farmer Jones. Her humility and obedience,
her piety, her capacity for love, forgiveness and gratitude, her chari-
ties, and the regulation of her married life all throw out the challenge
of an old-fashioned morality to a frivolous and lax society. The scenes
of choric praise enact Richardson's hopes for the educative power of
his story. They also prefigure the idea of moral community which is
central to *Sir Charles Grandison*. The living example and the public
discussion of virtue awaken the latent good nature and moral sensibility of all who meet them. All are "improved"; and in joining the
concord of praise all find their true selves, and the true sense of
fellowship binding them to their neighbours.

It remains unfortunatey true that it is not merely the overt didacticism of all this that prevents Richardson's readers from making the
same response. For the novel, although it is not a case-study of hypocrisy, still fails in several important ways.

The most central of these concerns not Pamela but B. Once one
has learned to read with the sensitivity to implications that Richardson demands, it becomes clear that after markedly crude beginnings B.
thus become a complex character in the grip of acute conflict. But if
Pamela and B. are both on the stage, and we are required to understand and judge them both in their opposition, the fact remains that
we live always in her mind and never in his because the novel is told
from a single point of view. Not only is it fatally easy to miss the exact
fluctuations of B.'s conflict through superficial reading, but we in-
habit so continuously a mind in which he appears simply as a "black-
hearted wretch" that we tend to oversimplify him too. (It is always
a danger in point-of-view writing that we are tempted to adopt the
viewpoint of one character instead of holding them all against our
own greater knowledge.) At important points we need the same direct
experience of B.'s heart and mind that we have of Pamela's; but the
single focus cannot provide this. The result is disastrous when we
come to B.'s reformation. If we are reading carefully enough we
should understand perfectly clearly why and how it happens, but we
cannot *experience* it. It is not proved on our pulses, it cannot have the

imaginative reality of Pamela's transformation. If we do not grasp the technical origin of this, or are reading carelessly anyway, our response is likely to register itself in doubts of the quality of Pamela's forgiveness, her return, her gratitude and meekness, which ought never to have arisen. Critics who believe that it is not the man she objected to all along, but his terms, ought to be discussing not Pamela but B., and not B. as Richardson intended him, but his realization. Yet, however technical, this is a serious failure that affects one's whole response to the novel.

There are also flaws which are the result of crude moral vision, and most have to do with Richardson's attitude to sex. He is frequently accused of prurience. Any honest reader knows, however, that the sexual scenes are anything but inflammatory. Yet there is something strange about them, and this is that they are not *about* sex at all. They are intensifications of a study of pride, theatrical attempts of the male to subjugate, and they result in humiliation. They remain unsatisfactory, not because Richardson gives too much treatment to sex, but too little; because he treats it too narrowly in its brutally egotistic and violating aspects, and sees too little of its full human potential and significance. There are, however, once again interesting signs in Pamela's reactions to her wedding night, and in her attitude towards Sally Godfrey and her child, of the dawnings of more liberal attitudes.

Again, in putting virtue on trial in a sexual arena, Richardson has a tendency to confuse virtue with physical virginity. Towards the end Pamela becomes clear that her integrity would be untouched by violation, but earlier Richardson had allowed her to speak of the attempts at rape as though these had been her worst trials. This could only be true physically and emotionally; the hardest tests of her whole being come in the scenes where her own unacknowledged love and B.'s gentleness combine to trouble her. In these scenes Richardson's vision is clean and sure; but his tendency to give undifferentiated praise to her "resistance" too often leaves the assumption open that he places as much emphasis on resistance to force and finance as on the far deeper values which first send Pamela into the wilderness, and then bring her back to her master in love and faith. There is a similar crudity, less of the imaginative creation than of the author's attitude towards it, in the concept of virtue rewarded which gives *Pamela* its subtitle. Though calculating prudence is one of Pamela's faults, perhaps the greatest achievement of the novel is the way in which the fault is transcended. Yet in his subtitle and the moral summary he appended, Richardson does fall back into crudity, and appears to argue as though the reasons for being virtuous had something to do with the calculation of rewards. Pamela is not a hypocritical politician, but she could legitimately blame her creator if readers are tempted to foist upon her the idea that virginity is the best policy.

Indeed Richardson's value is vitally dependent on his dramatic imagination. The significance of *Pamela* is precisely the way in which he was able to feel his way imaginatively towards deeper and finer attitudes. Flaws remain, but they are less important than the growth. Yet the sequel to the novel shows again how fatally easy it was for him to relapse as soon as his dramatic imagination no longer predominated. He had finished his work, but to meet the challenge of an unscrupulous hack who advertised a sequel, he forced himself to continue. Apart from some technical experiment and a wholly proper realization that the reformation of B. had come rather too easily, the book is a product of the didactic will rather than the creative imagination. It shows all too clearly the pressure of the regid, calculating morality he had inherited. Yet it also shows, by contrast with the first novel, the great value of the imagination which had enabled him to transcend himself as long as it continued to operate. What we watch in *Pamela*, despite its flaws, is the invention of a kind of novel which can help its author to find his way to a deeper sense of human integrity and a nobler idea of how human beings can attain true relationship with one another and with God. This seems more important than the faults of his first attempt.

Richardson and the Bold Young Men

by Morris Golden

By and large, Samuel Richardson has been lucky in his critics, from his own day to ours. A wide circle of disciples admired the usefulness of his morality, Johnson praised his analytical brilliance, Diderot eulogized his superhuman knowledge of the springs of human action, and even Fielding, his most conspicuous rival, found his major work overpowering. The criticism and scholarship since has been of unusually high quality. . . .

But despite all of this perceptive criticism, something remains to be said about the one aspect of Richardson's art which most fully distinguishes it from that of his predecessors and contemporaries—his view and communication of character. As a thinker he is negligible; as a technician he is important in the development of the epistolary novel, a form which has very few successes besides his own; as a social and literary commentator he is mediocre in his own right, though revealing as an unconscious reflecter of issues pervasive in his time, place, and class. But in his perception of the hidden bases of character—perception, not study, for his conscious study is on the level of the syndicated columnist of advice to the lovelorn—he seems to me unique in his time, a genuine precursor of Dostoevski and Lawrence, and their equal in intensity though not in coherence.

* * *

Even more than most novelists, Richardson is limited in his characters to a few staple types, which are stretched and chopped to fit various molds in his three novels. Unlike such writers as Fielding or Jane Austen in whose books character types recur, it is not Richardson's achievement, whatever his ostensible aim, to show certain intellectual or moral conceptions of human character working themselves out under differing circumstances. Rather, like Lawrence or Dostoevski or Faulkner, he seems to conceive of character as essentially passional; whatever moral arguments he claims to be making are purely superimposed, as witness

Reprinted from the "Preface" and "Richardson and the Bold Young Men" in Richardson's Characters *by Morris Golden, pp. vii–viii, 1–5, 6, 10, 11–14, 17–18, 23, 27–28, by permission of The University of Michigan Press. Copyright © 1963 by The University of Michigan Press.*

the great discrepancies between his editorial comments on the first two novels and the effect and nature of the novels themselves. For two hundred years critics have doubted Pamela's "signal veracity" and have questioned whether it was really her virtue that was rewarded; we suspect that *Clarissa* is not primarily a treatise on the enlightened governance of daughters or a homily against running off with rakes. We know that there is something else in these books, particularly the latter, that perennially fascinates us. As a number of critics have been arguing lately, it is the conflict of wills, even more of psyches, that gives these novels their power; and it seems to me, as it has seemed to others, that this direct perception of psychological reality derives from Richardson's own nature, which affected his view of the constitution of the society around him and impelled him to create his lurid emotional effects and his occasionally more lurid characters.

It was long believed, largely on the basis of Richardson's own claims, that he was unparalleled in drawing the hearts and minds of women, perhaps because, in Dobson's phrase, he was a "feminine man." [1] Latterly, much more emphasis has been placed on his self-identification with the rakish mental make-up (an emphasis which goes back with a minority of critics, like the Fielding of *Shamela*, to Richardson's earliest notices). David Daiches, perhaps too simply, says that Lovelace "is a mild and timid man's picture of the ideal rake, of Satan as gentleman, witty, boisterous, adventurous, courageous, ruthless"; [2] Ian Watt, whose insight into Richardson's mind in this instance seems to me the most perceptive, believes that the treatment of the fallen women in the first two novels (to which may be added that of Lord W.'s mistress in *Sir Charles Grandison*), "the fact that both these novels require the tacit assumption that the passions of his heroines are aroused by rakes, together with his own interest in fallen women and in the 'Magdalen Charity'—all these suggest an obsessional interest in criminal sexuality, an incompletely mastered striving for the kind of experience that 'Mr. B.' and Lovelace represent. It is likely that Richardson had a deep unconscious investment in his hero's sadistic attempts to violate Clarissa. . . ." [3] Richardson does have this "deep unconscious investment," and it manifests itself in his most interesting young men characters—not only the bad ones, like Lovelace, his pale shadows in *Sir Charles Grandison* (Sir Hargraves Pollexfen, Greville, and Fenwick), and the earlier Mr. B., but also in the model of philanthropic gentility, Sir Charles Grandison himself.

[1] Austin Dobson, *Samuel Richardson*, English Men of Letters (London: Macmillan, 1902), p. 36.

[2] *Literary Essays* (New York: Philosophical Library, 1957), p. 48.

[3] "The Naming of Characters in Defoe, Richardson, and Fielding," *RES*, XXV (1949), 333.

By extension, the same preoccupation pervades Richardson's whole view of character, of whatever sex, position, or age. In a letter to his Dutch admirer and translator Stinstra Richardson wrote: "Men and women are brothers and sisters; they are not of different species; and what need be obtained to know both, but to allow for different modes of education, for situation and constitution, or perhaps I should rather say, for habits, whether good or bad." [4] Though no law requires novelists to phrase exactly the theories of character which they have used, or even to have such theories, this is an extremely important passage. It suggests that for Richardson, preeminent at least in his time for the delineation of the distinction between the sexes, this distinction was essentially made by society and upbringing; that the constituents of character that Richardson saw when he looked within himself are the constituent elements in all human beings; that life, if this is so, is at the bottom of the psyche a wild conflict for dominance; and that moral differences among people will depend on the degrees to which they can restrain the violence of their urges in the interest of social living. But, as I hope to show, for Richardson the merit of a character is not directly and only proportional to the degree of restraint; complete lack of restraint, as in Lovelace, is close to complete evil, but on the other hand even Lovelace is immensely attractive, and the ideally genteel Grandison achieves, with his author's complete approval, total dominance over the society around him. It is true that Grandison is much praised for repressing what he insists is a highly passionate nature, but it is important that Richardson does give him this nature and does make a point of letting him show it at times.

Of the variety of rakish traits which Richardson shared with his major male characters, the least objectionable socially was an aggravated tendency to study young women—a trait leading to his purported "mastery in the delineation of the female heart." When he was thirteen, as he wrote to Stinstra, he had been let into the secrets of the girls for whom he wrote love letters (*Correspondence,* V, 263–64). When he became famous and surrounded himself with a platonic harem of honorary daughters, he not only constituted himself a chief

[4] Samuel Richardson, *Correspondence,* ed. Anna Laetitia Barbauld (London: Richard Phillips, 1804), V, 263. This collection will hereafter be referred to as *Correspondence. Cf.* also a comment on Shakespeare in a letter to Lady Bradshaigh of February 14, 1754, a comment which the feminist Mrs. Barbauld seems to have crossed out when she prepared the letters for publication: "He knew them [women] better than they knew themselves; for, pardon me for saying, that we must not always go to women for a *general* knowledge of the Sex. Asks me now with disdain, my dear Lady B., if *I* pretend to know them? No, I say—I only guess at them: And yet I think them not such mysteries as some suppose. A tolerable knowledge of men will lead us to a tolerable knowledge of women." Forster Collection, Vol. XI.

dispenser of advice on all problems of the heart but also very consciously observed the girls in relation to himself (*Correspondence*, III, 222–25). He admitted, in a perceptive self analysis, that "it is inconceivable how much advantage, in my proud heart, is given me, of peeping into the hearts of my readers, and sometimes into their heads, by their approbation, and disapprobation, of the conduct of the different persons in my Drama. . . ." [5] His attitude toward the young women who were his preferred friends, as revealed both in his letters and in his novels, resembles that of a psychologist toward a particularly endearing lot of guinea pigs. The basic situations of the bold young men in the novels are very similar: Lovelace, the boldest and most powerful of them, keeps Clarissa under constant and predatory surveillance. Mr. B., who is not so persistent a watcher (he has a surrogate in Mrs. Jewkes), nonetheless admits that for months before his mother's death he had been steadily observing Pamela and waiting for her physical and emotional ripeness for seduction.

*   *   *

Many writers have commented on Richardson's sadistic treatment of his female characters. It is easy enough to document, in the big scenes which would now appear on the dust jackets of his books: Pamela howling as Mr. B. attempts rape, throwing herself at his knees at other times, fainting to the floor at his threats; Clarissa thrashing about the floor half naked begging Lovelace not to violate her, and later undergoing violation before a noisy audience of prostitutes; Harriet Byron gagged and struggling in Sir Hargraves' coach while her kidnapper leers, and afterwards, from the floor of Grandison's chariot, piteously crying for help. All four heroines (allowing for two in the last novel) are threatened with beatings and at times suffer them, sometimes gratuitously—Clarissa, for example, falls on her nose when a door that she is storming in her home is suddenly opened. The similarity to Richardson's own temperament in this respect is everywhere evident; moreover, he was himself aware of the connections between his sadistic fantasies, and his sort of art: on March 25, 1751, he wrote to Mrs. Sarah Chapone, "What a deal of Wickedness may it be infer'd was in my Mind to draw from *thence* such a Man as Lovelace:—Indeed I put the Iniquity of two or three bad Characters together in my Mind in order to draw his. . . ." [6]

*   *   *

If the bold young men are expressions of Richardson's fantasies, it is not surprising that the conspicuous ones among them have in

[5] Letter to Lady Bradshaigh, February 14, 1754, in Forster Collection of MSS at the Victoria and Albert Museum, Vol. XI (Vol. I of the Richardson MSS).

[6] Forster Collection, Vol. XII.

common a manner which makes women come to them despite their lordliness—the full desire of the sadist is not satisfied until the girl both loves and fears, until she is hurt but continues loving nonetheless, or perhaps even as a consequence. Pamela, after Mr. B. has attempted her bosom, wants to leave partly because she is not sure that she can withstand his temptations;[7] after he has tried to rape her, had her kidnapped, and placed the odious Mrs. Jewkes over her, she hears that he has nearly drowned while hunting and thinks, "O what an Angel would he be in my Eyes yet, if he would cease his Attempts, and reform" (I, 243). Adding intolerable insult, he sends up to her prison room proposals for making her his mistress, to which she answers, "I know not the Man breathing I would wish to marry; and . . . the only one I could honour more than another, is the Gentleman, who, of all others, seeks my ever-lasting Dishonour" (I, 257); after the next rape attempt, "now I begin to be afraid, I know too well the Reason why all his hard Trials of me, and my black Apprehensions, would not let me hate him" (I, 294). As much as Pamela, B. has his cake and eats it—not only the pleasure of torturing her, but also the satisfaction of gaining her love.

*   *   *

In view of this sadistic element in their constitutions, it is not surprising that all of the bold young men characters (echoing Richardson's own domestic arrangements, though in an exaggerated way) wish to maintain dominance over their women, wish to be their sole supports, wish to have the women's exclusive regard, both in the future and retroactively. Here, despite the complex analyses of Richardson's social thought which have recently been made by Daiches, Watt, McKillop, and Fiedler, is the prime reason for the uniformly superior social positions of the male lovers in the novels over the female ones: the make-up of Richardson's mind is far more important in determining these positions on the basis of a fantasy of dominance than is some scheme of symbolism involving the relations between the aristocracy and the bourgeoisie. Though an endearing quality of *Pamela* is the heroine's triumph over her lover, Mr. B. is frequently seen in positions of physical mastery over Pamela. He stands over her while she cries on the floor (I, 248); he orders her to wait on him at table, attending behind him "out of my sight": "Sir, said I, and clasp'd his Knees with my Arms, not knowing what I did, and falling on my Knees, Have Mercy on me, and hear me, concerning that Wicked Woman's usage of me—" (I, 251). When he finally proposes marriage he is accepted in language which is most soothing

[7] Samuel Richardson, *Pamela, or, Virtue Rewarded*, Shakespeare Head Ed. (Oxford: Blackwell, 1929), I, 46. Subsequent references to *Pamela* are to this edition.

to his ego and to that of his creator: ". . . I hope it will be always my Pride to glory most in your Goodness; and it will be a Pleasure to me to shew every one, that, with respect to my Happiness in this Life, I am intirely the work of your Bounty; and to let the World see from what a lowly Original you have raised me to Honours that the greatest Ladies would rejoice in" (II, 42). The wedding ceremony pays due regard to the fantasies of dominance: B. said afterwards "That when he had done saying, *With this Ring I thee wed,* &c. I made a Court'sy, and said, Thank you, Sir" (II, 144). The next day she is grateful first to B. and then to God, and hopes "that I may preserve an humble and upright Mind to my gracious God, a dutiful Gratitude to my dear Master and Husband. . . ." (II, 165–66); and though Pamela is amused by the forty-eight rules for her behavior as a wife that Mr. B. lays down, she nonetheless accepts them. The refractory attitude of Lady Davers further enables B. to show his dominance; and although his actions are childish, Pamela is forced to consider them seriously, the point being that even an irrational husband is to rule: "Presuming *Pamela!* replied he, and made me start, Art thou then so hardy, so well able to sustain a Displeasure, which, of all things, I expected, from thy Affection, and thy Tenderness, thou wouldst have wished to avoid? . . . And, *Pamela,* I'll forgive you too, if you do not again make my Displeasure so light a thing to you, as you did just now" (II, 271–73).

B. was himself aware of his need to be unquestioned ruler, and had once said to Sir Simon Darnford that "he thought he should hardly have made a tolerable Husband to any body but *Pamela*" (III, 73), since he must have his way and be the superior. Reporting on his having frightened Pamela when she attempted to manipulate his attitude toward his bastard daughter, B. takes a typical dominance-fantasy view of her: "What have I done? Let me know, dear good Sir! looking round, with her half affrighted Eyes, this way and that, on the Books, and Pictures, and on me, by Turns. . . . I still held one Hand, and she stood before me, as Criminals ought to do before their Judge. . . ." (III, 132); the attitude is much like Lovelace's, though the situation is even more repellently sadistic, since it is arranged purely for fun. In the only continuous argument between the couple, over whether Pamela should suckle her young, B. has his own dominance in the family in mind in his objections: he admits that he would be jealous of Pamela's being distracted by his own child and does not want to be awakened at night when she feeds it. Miss Darnford, observing the B.'s at the time of the first childbirth, writes that B. "is lofty, and will not be disputed with; but I never saw a more polite and tender Husband, for all that" (IV, 127).

*   *   *

The pervasiveness of fantasy in the creation of character is, I believe, Richardson's preeminent contribution to the novel; and the
fantasies are mainly of dominance and subordination, as seem to have
been those of the author himself. Lovelace is the most conspicuous
weaver of fantasies, but both the major men and women partake in
them—sometimes through transparent dreams, sometimes in inco-
herent raving, sometimes in more or less rational elaborations of plans,
and sometimes by virtue of their situations as actors of the fantasy in
Richardson's mind. Mr. B. even has his fantasy detailed by his early
female alter ego, Mrs. Jewkes, who tells Pamela that he "has found
out a way to satisfy my Scruples: It is, by marrying me to this dreadful
Colbrand, and buying me of him on the Wedding-day, for a Sum of
Money! . . . She says it will be my Duty to obey my Husband; and
that Mr. *Williams* will be forced, as a Punishment, to marry us. . . .
But this, to be sure, is horrid romancing!" (I, 243–44). In the garden
scene which prefigures B.'s reform, he insists on having the remainder
of Pamela's journal (her most secret thoughts must conform to his
dream of himself as her master); at her refusal to tell where it is, he
proposes to strip her in search of it, promising himself considerable
amusement. Pamela, no martyr, provides the papers immediately.

*   *   *

As a concomitant to the sadism either exhibited by the bold young
men in their thirst for dominance or implied in their actions, situations, or dreams, these characters show also, like their creator, the com-
plementary guilt feelings that at times are extreme enough to constitute masochism. Again Lovelace, Richardson's prime psychotic, most
clearly manifests this symptom, but the others also have traces. Mr. B.,
for example, takes a curious pride in having Pamela tell his genteel
circle about his mischievous and malicious actions (II, 104); he assures
her, after their marriage, that she is his superior mentally (II, 152); he
describes how, while planning her seduction, he had despised himself
(III, 207); and several times he enjoys reading repentantly those passages in Pamela's diaries and letters in which she has described his
viciousness (e.g., IV, 199).

*   *   *

. . . I argue, therefore, that Richardson's most lively and effective
male characters are modifications, sometimes great and sometimes
minor, of certain urges, rather than rational actors chosen for moral
or artistic reasons. In his attractive characters, Richardson finds the
urge to violence as important as its judicious restraint. Without this
urge, men are shown as colorless and faintly absurd. The men with
the urge toward dominance achieve the heroines; those without it,
consolation prizes of dubious value.

Moralists, Novelists, and Unfallacious Intentions

by Sheldon Sacks

It is only the mildest hyperbole to assert that those who write about Richardson and Fielding feel impelled to become semi-exclusive partisans of one or the other. Critics as diverse in point of view of time and interests as Samuel Johnson and Ian Watt, for example, seem sensitive almost exclusively to the merits of one of the two novelists. My purpose is not to reconcile, explain, or take sides in the persistent controversy. But in refuting one assumption made by some of their present-day partisans about the conscious moral and aesthetic intentions of the two novelists, I may more decisively lay my two ghosts and simplify the complicated reason for rejecting both of their polar formularizations of the relation between a novelist's ethical convictions and the form of the novel he writes.

The formularization most difficult for me to deal with, because it is more in accord with my own critical prejudices, is that which presumes that, because Fielding was not "writing a system" but a novel, inferences about his beliefs can at best be minimal; that devices of disclosure making us feel admiration or contempt, sympathy or aversion, for acts and statements of the cowboys or the Indians, the cops or the robbers, the Blifils or the Joneses, may have a purely accidental relation to the writers' ethical convictions, since the purpose of these formal signals is to ensure that the readers' emotional reactions at any given point are consonant with the total effect the whole work is designed to produce.

The second formularization is not so difficult to refute on theoretical as on practical grounds. As an unstated assumption it underlies many critiques which adduce evidence of writers' beliefs from their works in an offhand manner; the ease with which it apparently enables us

"Moralists, Novelists, and Unfallacious Intentions." From Chapter Six, "The Great, Useful, and Uncommon Doctrine" in Fiction and the Shape of Belief: A Study of Henry Fielding with Glances at Swift, Johnson, and Richardson, by Sheldon Sacks (Berkeley: University of California Press, 1964; London: Cambridge University Press, 1964), pp. 234–41. Copyright © by the Regents of the University of California. Reprinted by permission of the University of California Press.

to relate knowledge derived from studies in biography or the history of ideas to literary works has made teaching procedures dependent upon its validity disquieting favorites in university classrooms. It embodies the assumption that most, possibly all, literary works exemplify themes: literary structure itself is a matter of the relationship of a main theme[1] and subsidiary themes to each other and to the actions which exemplify them. In *Tom Jones*, for example, Fielding's "doctrine, which it is the purpose of this whole work to inculcate," is presumably the organizing theme which the actions of the characters exemplify. If we accept this notion, an attempt to consider local evaluations apart from their relation to Fielding's doctrine would be as fruitless as an attempt to consider the parts of *Rasselas* without reference to Johnson's formally controlling statement about the pursuit of earthly happiness. Indeed, if we accept this view, we must conclude that all literary works are organized as mere variations of the structure ascribed to *Rasselas*; the particular controlling themes and the ways in which they are exemplified account for the differences among literary works.

Accept tentatively the first of the two polar views, which assumes that the judgments conveyed by a novelist are dictated by the form of his work; an immediate consequence is that, if we admire *Tom Jones*, we must regard Fielding's statements of his moral intentions with suspicion; we may write them off as sops to an audience which expected moral apologia, as evidence that writers are not conscious of what they have really done, as subsidiary purposes which fortunately did not prevent Fielding from achieving the requisite artistic end; or we may simply ignore their existence. More moderate forms of this polar view seem to underlie some descriptions of the difference between Fielding's and Richardson's contributions to the development of the novel; it is common to regard Richardson as primarily and consciously a moralist who accidentally made important contributions to the new genre, in contradistinction to Fielding, who was a novelist first and a moralist, if at all, incidentally. A well-known American critic states: "Richardson, who, though not without artistic merit, was primarily a moralist, brought the gift of psychological insight to the novel; Fielding, despite uncertainties of handling in *Joseph Andrews*, described and demonstrated the form."[2] There is considerable, though I should argue only ostensible, historical and biographical support for such a view. Fielding's own famous attacks on *Pamela*, for example, are primarily attacks on the morality he thought the

---

[1] I do not imply that the word "theme" is used only in this way; its uses are multifarious.

[2] Howard Mumford Jones in his introduction to *Joseph Andrews* (New York: Modern Library College Editions, 1950), p. vii.

work embodied, and, since the twentieth-century reader who is at all likely to read *Pamela* is not likely to share Richardson's views about the importance of virginity, Fielding's attacks seem apt. On the other hand, although Richardson's objections to Fielding and his work are made on moral grounds, the same reader who rejected Richardson's morality in the first place may be expected to regard his objections as further evidence that he is primarily a moralist, and not a very appealing one at that. Since Fielding's moral attack on *Pamela* seems apt, but Richardson's moral attacks on Fielding and his novels seems irrelevant, the view that Fielding's work is primarily "art" and Richardson's primarily morality gains delusive support.

The consequences of adopting such a view are so significant . . . that we should be wary of accepting it. Once assume *Pamela* is a work of morality, once ignore Fielding's statements of moral purpose or assume that they are supererogatory, and—though we might quibble about definition—we can hardly object when the same well-known critic concludes that *Joseph Andrews* is "the first English novel consciously fulfilling an aesthetic theory." [3]

But if, for the sake of argument, we make the far less drastic assumption that both novelists were sincere in their statements of purpose but that such statements may not automatically be interpreted as analyses of the literary types in which their purposes are embodied, we may, simply by selecting arbitrarily from among those statements, not only convict Fielding of being primarily a moralist, but accuse Richardson of writing *Pamela* to fulfill an almost decadently aesthetic purpose. We need not bother to prosecute Fielding at length, since all that is necessary to convict him is to remind the reader of the blatantly moral statements in the opening pages of each of his three major novels. But convicting Richardson of hedonism on the basis of clearly expressed statements from the preface to *Pamela* is important for the remainder of this section and is good sport as well. Among the "desirable Ends" which he claims are "obtained in these Sheets" are the following:

> to Divert and Entertain
> to draw Characters justly, and to support them equally
> to raise a Distress from natural Causes, and to excite Compassion from proper Motives
> to effect all these good Ends, in so probable, so natural, so lively a manner, as shall engage the Passions of every sensible Reader.[4]

Indeed, even in his summary of the ends achieved in *Pamela*, he is unable to resist a parenthetical glance at Pan and assures us: "If

[3] *Ibid.*, p. vi.
[4] Samuel Richardson's "Introduction to *Pamela*," ed. Sheridan W. Baker (Los Angeles: Augustan Reprint Society, 1954), pp. iii, iv, v.

these (embellished with a great Variety of entertaining Incidents) be laudable or worthy Recommendations of any Work, the Editor of the following Letters, which have their Foundation in Truth and Nature, ventures to assert, that all these desirable Ends are obtained in these Sheets." [5]

To isolate these remarks from the blatantly moral context in which they appear is to distort Richardson's intentions, but not to a greater degree than we distort them by wrenching his moral statements from their aesthetic context; there is no reason to believe that those nonmoral aims are any less sincere than the moral aims. If we ignore either the moral or aesthetic purposes, we argue from so partial a truth that, whether we try to describe Richardson's role in the development of the English novel or attempt to infer his beliefs from *Pamela*, we will go as far astray as if what we had assumed were absolutely false.

We can see this more clearly if we recognize that one aspect of our well known critic's argument is quite justified: Richardson did have a blatantly moral intention when he wrote *Pamela*.[6] But, since we wish to know whether the primacy of his moral purpose could have prevented Richardson from writing "the first English novel consciously fulfilling an aesthetic theory," we must still determine in what type of fiction he could have embodied his moral intention and still have achieved the nonmoral aims listed in the preface to *Pamela*. It is sufficient to ask initially whether he could have written a work of prose fiction which achieved those aims and was, at the same time, structurally analogous to *Rasselas*—a work organized to exemplify an idea or a closely related set of ideas.

Such a work is clearly incompatible with those aims. If one writes prose fiction in which he really attempts "to raise a Distress from natural Causes, and to excite Compassion from proper Motives," if he attempts to "support [characters] equally," if he is intensely concerned with literary probability, he has introduced another set of criteria for the selection, ordering, and manner of representing episodes; it becomes virtually impossible for him simultaneously to select, order, and represent those episodes in such a way that they will demonstrate the truth or falsity of a single concept or a closely related set of concepts. If Johnson had aimed at even one of those conditions —to excite compassion from proper motives—he might indeed have made use of an Oriental setting, and of a different character named Rasselas whose attempt to find happiness had failed, and might indeed have caused us to feel distress at that failure, but he could hardly have done so and retained the highly general representation of his

---

[5] *Ibid.*, pp. v–vi.

[6] But, it should be remembered, not in opposition to Fielding, whom we may regard as a self-convicted moralist.

protagonist, nor that particular kind of "chance" relation of episodes in which the protagonist and his friends just happen to meet a series of characters who, though barely delineated, happen perfectly to exemplify potential modes of happiness which immediately turn out to be false. He could no longer retain that series of episodes—though their inclusion in the *Rasselas* Johnson wrote is quite effective—in which Pekuah, characterized only as a maid loyal to the hero's sister and afraid of ghosts, is carried off by an unknown Arab so that, ransomed, she may return to tell a tale which conveniently illustrates the lack of happiness in a culture not directly explored by the hero.

No matter how moral Johnson's purpose, no matter how strongly he wishes us to share his opinion that the earthly hope we pursue is a phantom, the moment he decides to make Richardson's nonmoral aims the conditions of his prose fiction, he commits himself in advance to choices among mutually exclusive literary forms and the *Rasselas* we know becomes impossible. His conviction about happiness may—and if the novel he writes is of reasonable scope, undoubtedly will—be expressed in those devices of disclosure which make us feel as we do about the characters, actions, and thoughts represented in his fiction, but the whole work cannot be organized as an exemplification of that conviction.

If we agree that *Rasselas* is an excellent work of its kind, we cannot wish Johnson had made the sorts of changes enumerated above, though these changes and many others would be necessary to fulfill the nonmoral aims of *Pamela*. We must conclude, then, that if two men have equally strong moral purposes when writing prose fictions, but one has assumed certain minimal aims which we associate with novels as conditions of his own work, the forms they create will be so different from each other that similar criteria for excellence cannot be fruitfully applied to both. *Rasselas* is a disjointed novel, but an excellent apologue.* If Richardson successfully embodied his moral purpose in a work that achieved his nonmoral aims, he may have produced an excellent novel, but it must be a very poorly constructed apologue. Since both Richardson and Fielding did have moral purposes in writing their novels, and Richardson did have conscious nonmoral aims of such a nature that their successful achievement would automatically

---

* [Mr. Sacks organizes his discussion of prose fiction on these three types:

A satire is a work organized so that it ridicules objects external to the fictional world created in it.

An apologue is a work organized as a fictional example of the truth of a formulable statement or a series of such statements.

An action is a work organized so that it introduces characters, about whose fates we are made to care, in unstable relationships which are then further complicated until the complication is finally resolved by the removal of the represented instability.]

result in what we now call a novel, we can hardly agree that *Joseph Andrews* is "the first English novel consciously fulfilling an aesthetic theory."

Unless human nature had undergone a complete transformation since Richardson's time and made it impossible for us to read *Pamela* at all, the villagers who rang church bells on learning of the fictional heroine's marriage to her would-be seducer were hardly likely to have been celebrating their reinforced moral convictions that an able preservation of chastity will be materially rewarded; their reaction to Pamela's marriage to her erstwhile seducer could only result from her creator's successful efforts at drawing characters justly and supporting them equally, at raising a distress from natural causes and exciting compassion from proper motives, and from the fact that he achieved these ends in so probable, so natural, so lively a manner that he did indeed engage the passions of sensible readers. One can hardly imagine bells being rung for the safe return of Pekuah! Only the insensitive, or a shrewd writer of burlesque, could interpret *Pamela* as an exemplification of the notion that a cunning preservation of virtue, defined as virginity, will be rewarded, when its heroine is capable of writing:

> I shall make a fine figure with my singing and dancing when I come home! I shall be unfit for a *May-day* holiday; for these minuets, rigadoons, and French dances . . . will make me but ill company for my milk-maid companions that are to be. I had better, as things are, have learned to wash, scour, brew, bake, and such like. But I hope, if I can't get work, and can meet with a place, to learn these soon, if any body will have the goodness to bear with me till I am able. . . . It may be a little hard at first; but woe to my proud heart if I find it so on trial! I will make it bend to its condition or break it.[7]

Obviously Pamela does preserve her chastity and obviously she is rewarded; this does not mean that she represents virtue rewarded. The girl represented in the quoted passage as looking almost with horror on her return, although with maidenhead intact, to her milk-maid companions is hardly an appropriate central figure for an apologue; she is a highly characterized fifteen-year-old girl who has emerged from poverty to live on the fringes of a world of great affluence; she is conscious that she has been spoiled for the world in which she was born, but she has a moral sensibility which prevents her from assuming the role of a paid mistress and has but one commodity, her attractive body, with which to gain permanent entrée into the only world in which she is now fit to live.

This is not to say that Richardson did not feel or try to make his reader feel that his harassed heroine was virtuous; on the contrary, un-

[7] Samuel Richardson, *Pamela* (New York: E. P. Dutton and Co., 1949), pp. 62–63.

less he can convince his reader that she does act virtuously in the situation in which she is placed, *Pamela* cannot be artistically successful. One of those circumstances is, of course, her understandable desire not to return to impoverished rural life. Fail to take into account the resolution necessary for her to return to this life, and her reluctance to get home when, ostensibly, she is still free to do so, defines her as a kind of Shamela. Fail to take into account that when she has won Mr. B. she has not automatically won herself a place in the only world in which she is now fit to live, and the part of the novel representing her activities after marriage becomes artistically superfluous; [8] if Richardson had actually created a sister to Shamela, all expectations would have been resolved when she won Mr. B., but Pamela must win over her husband's family and friends or she has lost all.

That Pamela is meant to be seen as virtuous is not in question. That Richardson had sincere moral intentions in writing the book is not in doubt. Once admit, however, that we must take into account such considerations as those above when we discuss *Pamela*, that her "problems" and their artistic resolution issue in large part from her character, and that Richardson's conscious aesthetic aims indicate that this state of affairs was not the result of accident, and you have also admitted that, in writing *Pamela*, Richardson is primarily a novelist. The "morality" of the book is no longer as simple or accessible as it might appear, and any attempt to isolate it must depend on a series of inferences about what Richardson must have believed in order to evaluate as he did the characters, actions, and thoughts represented in the work, and especially to evaluate Pamela's actions with regard to the particular choices possible for such a character in such circumstances.

[8] I am not referring here to Richardson's sequel, but to the original novel, in which Pamela's adventures after her marriage occupy about one-fourth of the whole; her troubles with Mr. B.'s family begin even before her marriage.

Richardson's *Pamela:*
The Aesthetic Case

A. M. Kearney

Few novels have suffered so much at the hands of the critics as Richardson's *Pamela*. Its ambivalent moral attitudes and prurient content attracted plenty of abuse in its own day, and Arnold Kettle probably echoes a majority opinion in our own time when he writes: "*Pamela* remains only as a record of a peculiarly loathsome aspect of bourgeois puritan morality." [1]

This kind of verdict doubtless arises from a close preoccupation with the character of the heroine herself, and certainly her case is by no means a simple one either psychologically or morally as is testified by the extraordinary amount of interest shown in her. But this attempt to sabotage the motivation behind Pamela's conduct, set in motion by Fielding and other contemporary satirists of Richardson's work, provides only the narrowest and most dubious approach to the novel, which, as a highly original mode of writing in a new genre, deserves another kind of treatment. In fact *Pamela* turns out to be a much more interesting achievement than might be thought, and illustrates for us many of the problems inherent in the art of fiction itself and, in particular, the special problems of style and narration that exist in the epistolary technique. If the vexed question of Pamela's psychological motivation can be laid on one side and the novel can be regarded as an artistic whole we may, by looking at *Pamela* afresh in this way be able to disentangle Richardson's version from Fielding's.

Perhaps the most crucial problem raised by *Pamela* and certainly one which exercised Richardson throughout his life as a novelist, concerns the relationship between the "experience" of the novel—i.e. what actually takes place—and its emergent literary shape. While

---

"Richardson's Pamela: *The Aesthetic Case" by A. M. Kearney. From* The Review of English Literature, *VII (July, 1966), 78–90. Copyright © 1966 by Longman's Green & Co., Ltd. Reprinted by permission of the author and the editor, A. Norman Jeffares.*

[1] *An Introduction to the English Novel* (1951), I, 69.

this may present all writers of fiction with a special problem, to none is it so acute as to the epistolary novelist, where literature is created on the spot and out of the moment itself. In epistolary fiction, we watch the actual process of literature being made as private experience is transmuted into public knowledge. In this way, literary style becomes much more than surface manner, and the way the narrator treats of her experience is revelatory to a high degree, thus giving an interpretative power to epistolary style. In *Pamela*, particularly, the whole problem is heightened by the fact that the bulk of the writing is carried on by the chief participant herself, and the reader is placed in the position of not knowing the degree of correspondence between what is written down, and what actually happened. With a novelist like Fielding, of course, the problem does not arise: the author is always on hand to supply an authoritative commentary. When Tom Jones, for example, gets drunk on Allworthy's recovery, he has Fielding to explain away his behaviour, but when Pamela returns to Mr. B.'s after he has let her go, she has her own explaining to do. The result is that while Tom's character is an open book to us, Pamela's, as the critics have always insisted, is not. All this perhaps is fairly obvious, but it serves to show the particular narrative problem which faced Richardson in *Pamela*, and provides us with a convenient starting point for examining the complex relationship between experience and the literary product in the epistolary novel.

In reality we have two attitudes toward experience in this novel: Pamela's, and Richardson's own authorial one which he expresses through her. Pamela, in fact, is both "character" and "author" and the effect of this double function tends to make Pamela real at one moment and unreal the next; as an early critic claimed, she talks "like a *Philosopher* on one page and like a *changling* the next."[2] Corresponding with this double role, therefore, we have in effect two voices: the first manifesting itself in a direct and spontaneous manner, coming from the centre of experience itself, and the second a much more deliberate one, suggesting the impressions of the observer rather than the participant. In short, we have a voice which is recognizably Pamela's own, and a commentary which is often palpably not. But, before going on to consider the implications of this in greater detail, it will be as well to take a closer look at these voices in action and see the effect they have on the actual tempo of the novel.

The liveliest writing in the novel occurs in the early part, where Pamela's fear of physical outrage produces an almost instinctive recoil into words. This is where we have Pamela as distinct from the author speaking. Her descriptions of Mrs. Jewkes and Colbrand, for example,

[2] Cited by A. D. McKillop, *Samuel Richardson, Printer and Novelist*, Chapel Hill (1936), p. 67.

are nightmarish to the final detail: "she has a huge hand, and an arm as thick as my waist, I believe" (I, 99).[3] Colbrand's repulsiveness is similarly detailed: he had a "sword on, with a nasty red knot to it . . ." (I, 148–9). This is the least sophisticated of Pamela's styles— the instinctive *cri de coeur*—and comes from the field of action rather than the study. In the description of Colbrand, running in pursuit, "with his long legs, well nigh two yards at a stride" (I, 161), there is something elemental, and we have in its very "unliterariness" the suggestion of the experience itself rather than a delayed retrospect as elsewhere.

In marked contrast to this kind of thing, at other times even in the early part, we have a much more deliberate literary recording of events where, at first sight anyway, the style seems to distort rather than reflect the dramatic situation. In part this can be accounted for by recalling that Pamela's head was full of allusions culled from her wide reading, and these quite spontaneously take shape on the page as she writes. Thus she instinctively falls into Miltonic phrases like "brown nodding horrors" when describing the gloomy Lincolnshire trees (I, 94), or more frequently the biblical, as when comparing her chastity to the city assaulted by the sons of Edom (I, 293); particularly when she feels the need to relate her problems to a wider and more comforting context. In a similar way, her quoting *Hamlet* (I, 20), and her describing the edge of the carp-pond—in which she nearly drowned herself—as "these perilous banks" (I, 155), and Mr. B.'s falling into a stream whilst hunting as "the peril of perishing in deep waters" (I, 172), can be related to the kind of therapy effected by hyperbolic utterance. But such explanations quickly break down when we try to relate many of Pamela's reflections to the dramatic context which inspires them: no one similarly situated, we are forced to admit, would express themselves thus.

In these cases we have, quite unmistakably, the voice of Richardson himself, and the result is a kind of blurring in the characterization. (The same effect occurs in *Clarissa* as Richardson increasingly uses Belford as his mouthpiece.) At the same time, a sense of dramatic proportion is also lost on such occasions, and sometimes the effect is one of unconscious parody. (See, for example the passage where Pamela likens herself to Queen Hester, II, 305.) Sometimes, indeed, Richardson seems to counter his own intrusions into Pamela's writings by using other characters as critics of Pamela's style: Lady Davers, for example, takes Pamela to task when she neglects "truth and nature" for "studied or elaborate epistles" (II, 33), and Polly Darnford cautions her on the danger of "falling into a too thoughtful and gloomy way"

[3] All references to *Pamela* and *Clarissa* in this article are to the Everyman editions: 2 vols. 1914, and 4 vols. 1932, respectively.

of writing (II, 215). But the real fact of the matter is that Richardson
was prepared to sacrifice the strict demands of characterization in the
interests of his own entry into the novel. He was prepared to stick to
a psychological realism only so far, and his main concern was to im-
pose a deliberate and literary commentary upon the "raw event" and,
as a result, control it. Thus the second voice counters the first.

One of the chief reasons for this controlling technique can be related to the subject matter of the novel. Obviously the main theme
is a delicate one and Richardson found himself in considerable difficulties when trying to reform "young and airy minds" by attracting
them sufficiently in the first place. The danger was that they might
take away the wrong impressions. On the other hand, as he put it in a
letter to George Cheyne, "If I were to be too spiritual, I doubt I
should catch none but Grandmothers," though there were plenty
about "who cou'd find Sex in a *laced shoe*, when there was none in
the Foot, that was to wear it." [4] The alliance between the "inflaming"
and the "spiritual" in *Pamela* is perhaps an uneasy one, but certainly
one reason for the reaching after the formal style in Pamela's reflective
letters is an awareness on Richardson's part of its value as an intellectual counterweight. The effect on the reader is one of being involved in the experience and then abstracted from it and, ideally, one
has the best of both worlds.

In practice, of course, this is rarely the case, and Richardson found
that many of his readers were more taken with his villains than his
heroines. Nevertheless, the very literariness of the epistolary style,
which strengthens as the novel develops, tends to distance the "inflaming" content and to refine much of the pornography out of existence.
No one in fact was as conscious of indecency in literature as Richardson, though his very preoccupation with it suggests some ambivalence.
Both his letters and his novels are full of scathing references to "low"
authors (see for example, his remarks on Pope and Swift, *Selected
Letters*, p. 57, Clarissa's on Swift, IV, 504 and Pamela's on the "vile
epilogue" which concludes a particular performance of *The Distressed
Mother*, II, 259) and he obviously intends his own fiction as a correc-
tive to such writing.

Richardson's own writing however reveals a deep-rooted conflict
over this. The epistolary technique in his hands became a subtle prob-
ing instrument which sometimes opened the mind too far for comfort.
Lady Mary Wortley Montagu perfectly stated the Augustan case when,
with Richardson in mind, she remarked that "fig-leaves are as necessary for our minds as our bodies." [5] Richardson is pulled in both

[4] *Selected Letters of Samuel Richardson*, edited by John Carroll, Oxford (1964),
pp. 46–47.

[5] *Letters*, Everyman edition (1906), p. 466.

directions: his own inclination, and indeed talent as a writer, prompted him to release the (uncensored) contents of the mind in a flow of consciousness, but, at the same time, he is pulled away from the subjective pulse of experience towards the authorial and the objective which finally places him on the right side of the fence.

Pamela is especially interesting in that we can watch Richardson's first attempts to resolve these tensions in didactic art. In the early part, as we know, there is a wealth of lively involvement, but as the novel progresses a very different tone appears in Pamela's writings. She is still the sentient and moral centre of the novel but the author increasingly takes over. Her comments on masquerades, operas and the stage, as well as her lengthy treatment of Locke's theory of education, not only fairly represent Richardson's exact views, but indicate that the controlling voice is well inside the world of the novel. This shift in perspective from subjective to objective clearly suggests a change of function for the heroine, a change which parallels her elevation from low to high life.

While it would be untrue to say that Part II is nothing more than a weighty moral tract, what does happen is that much of the quickening power is lost as Pamela is more consciously "used" by the author. Richardson obviously found the lengthy process of retrospection that takes place in Part II a congenial task, and the whole performance is rather like the sermon in shape, where the *exemplum* is followed by an appropriate summary. But Part II is also in a sense an apology for Part I. As he takes pains to point out in his letters, "the poor scenes" —by which he means parts, especially in the early pages of the novel, likely to stimulate the passions—were intended "only for a *first Attractive.*" [6] The apology is rather a facile one, but Richardson clearly felt happier about the novel after completing the last two volumes, and was pleased to defend the lack of vitality in the second part by stating that in the interests of instruction, "I labour'd hard to rein in my Invention. . . ." [7] The term "invention" came to have unlawful connotations for Richardson as his sense of caution strengthened, and he was very grateful to the "kind Anonymous Gentleman" who vindicated scenes in *Pamela* which appeared too "deep" for nice readers, by pointing out in Milton "Passages full as strong if not stronger." [8]

The tensions that lie just beneath the surface in Richardson's novels are an interesting manifestation not only of the conflicts which existed in the author's own mentality, but of tensions that can be found at large in the literature of the period. "The Copernican revolution in epistemology," as M. H. Abrams has termed it, which

[6] *Selected Letters,* p. 47.
[7] Ibid., p. 54.
[8] Ibid., p. 50.

took shape as a conflict between objective and subjective theories about art, and between the respective claims of imitation and originality in authors, obviously affected far more than the poetry of the period, though this has received the most attention with reference to aesthetic theory. Richardson's influence in this debate was of course minimal, but his ambivalent attitude towards originality in literature, clearly highlighted in the novels themselves, makes him something of a test case. As Ian Watt points out, he was responsible "for a general sharpening of Young's polemic (that is, in the *Conjectures*) in the direction of a new anti-classical hierarchy of literary values." [9] But while his own strength as a writer lay in the direction of the expressive and self-taught, he was clearly not prepared to take his originality very far: he saw the dangers in his path.

His real achievement in fiction rests on his ability to do brilliant portrayals of the mind under duress, calling forth its deepest fears and primitive associations, and connecting the reader with these in a remarkably effective way. His use of the dream or dreamlike associations, in suggesting significant hallucinatory effects, anticipates the interest shown by later novelists in unconscious association. (See for example, *Pamela*, I, 135, and *Clarissa*, I, 433.) There is little point in speculating how far Richardson might have taken fiction had he been writing in a different aesthetic and moral climate, or if he had decided to use the potentialities of the epistolary technique as a mind-opener to the full. But it is relevant in passing to note his attitude towards *Tristram Shandy*, the most original novel of the day. As he wrote to Bishop Hildesley, he approved of the sentiments of a certain lady who concluded:

> Unaccountable wildness; whimsical digressions; comical incoherencies; uncommon indecencies; all with an air of novelty. . . . But mark my prophecy, that by another season, this performance will be as much decryed, as it is now extolled . . . and yet another prophecy I utter, that this ridiculous compound will be the cause of many more productions, witless and humourless, perhaps, but indecent and absurd. . . .[10]

Indecencies apart, he is not impressed by Sterne's bold experiment and is alarmed by the example he may have set for would-be authors. While he may approve the spirit of Sterne's rebuttal of Horace—"for in writing what I have set about, I shall confine myself neither to his rules, nor to any man's rules that ever lived" [11]—Richardson shies away from the real implications of originality in fiction which Sterne exploited so brilliantly.

Such ambivalence tends to make Richardson's own performance an

[9] Ian Watt, *The Rise of the Novel* (1957), p. 247.
[10] *Selected Letters*, pp. 341–2.
[11] *Tristram Shandy*, Bk. 1, ch. IV.

uneasy one. Unlike Fielding and Sterne who were able to rest their
fiction on established and learned traditions, Richardson's own approach to the novel is a hesitant one. Despite the speed with which
Pamela was written, he was never quite happy about either his own
qualifications as a novelist, or the finished results. (See for example,
Selected Letters, pp. 158 and 245.) His frequent requests for advice
during the actual course of writing—advice rarely accepted however
—betray his need to bring things out in the open, to discuss and abstract what in reality is the author's private concern. We can see therefore, that with all his *penchant* for the individual and subjective
conscience in art, Richardson's ultimate concern was to relate this to
the plane of an acceptable impersonality: in the end, the personal
voice in his fiction—insistent and pleading though it is—is always
replaced by the frankly authorial one.

The formalization that takes place in the second part of *Pamela*
is precisely this process in operation and the epistolary medium, which
tuned us in to the inner rhythms of the heroine's experiences, becomes increasingly an instrument of reflective commentary. The action
continues, but the present is always seen against the background of the
past in a mood of increasing retrospection. Here Richardson was aided
by the extreme adaptability of the epistolary medium itself which
can vary between wide shifts in tempo: both personal thought and
public statement find their proper level of utterance in the letter
form. Moreover, by applying certain stylistic criteria Richardson is
able to bring the whole body of writing that forms the novel into
correspondence with the nature of the lessons communicated.

In adapting what is in essence a folk archetype to the existing social
conditions of his time, Richardson carefully preserves a balance between the ritualistic and the familiar concerns of daily life. On one
level, Pamela develops rather like an allegorical quality—as Miss
Goodwin sees it, the figure of Prudence itself (II, 480)—but on another, and more satisfactory, level perhaps she emerges as an exemplar
of various social types: "the prudent Wife, the affectionate and tender
Mother, . . . the sincere Friend, the charitable Steward to the Poor,
etc." [12] Pamela's trials, insofar as they continue in Part II, therefore
come to have a distinct social flavour: the area of hostile confrontation has been shifted from bedroom and closet to the drawing-room,
and Pamela's various demonstrations of superior strength are increasingly public. The point of these rituals is to prove a right to recognition on Pamela's part; a right not only moral, but social. Pamela's
moral superiority is amply highlighted in the first part of the novel,
now she must be accorded another kind of recognition: her claim to
be called "sister" and "Mrs. B." is a well-founded one, and Richardson

[12] *Selected Letters*, p. 46.

insists upon the connexion between her social and moral qualities. This is the point of the rather drawn-out scene where Sir Jacob Swynford, refusing to meet Pamela as Mrs. B., is deceived into thinking that she is Lady Jenny (II, 163–8). His final recognition of Pamela's real identity leads him to acknowledge her full right to her "exalted condition": "I don't wonder at my nephew's loving you!—And you call her sister, Lady Davers, don't you?—If you do, I'll own her for my niece" (II, 169).

Richardson's chief claim in *Pamela* is that not only can virtue be transferred to good effect from one social context to another, but that without civilized recognition virtue is powerless in terms of influence. He says considerable stress therefore on the value of social status—and in doing so placed an unfortunate second meaning on the phrase "virtue rewarded"—though he carefully tries to distinguish between the superficial and the well-considered implications of the concept. Hence the public and ceremonious nature of much of the second part where Pamela and Mr. B. play out their privileged role in social life, and Pamela's critical observations are increasingly adapted to the wider scene. What she has to say, however, at this later stage of the novel, appears in a stylistic form which itself takes root in the social milieu to which she now belongs. Epistolary style in fact provides Richardson with a unique reflector of social and moral circumstance.

In an age which attached such importance to the notion of literary decorum, endless opportunities were afforded for stylistic exploitation of one kind or another. *Tom Jones,* of course, amongst other things, is a brilliant exhibition of rhetorical extravagance carefully adapted to certain dramatic ends. Like Fielding, Richardson is also aware of the value of style as dramatic function. Unlike Fielding, however, who utilized his stylistic excursions to point various comic incongruities, Richardson was mainly concerned with the literary style as an expression of moral being. His interest in this relationship is indicated by the many discussions of it in his letters and novels. The whole thing seems to turn on the question of unaffected deliberation, and Richardson's demands for epistolary style are as strongly realized as his rigorous requirements for any other form of conscious self-expression. We have in his novels therefore an insistence on a relationship between literary expression and moral value that hardly exists elsewhere.

In a world where such criteria exists, it is hardly surprising to find that Richardson's heroines have much to offer on the subject. Pamela is quick to censure Miss Stapylton's "allegorical or metaphorical style" because it strays too far from what is "easy, natural and unaffected" (II, 456) while Clarissa in connecting epistolary style with "judgment and discretion" goes so far as to detail several kinds of stylistic abuse (IV, 494–6). However, perhaps the clearest statement which concerns this relationship comes in *Grandison* where Charlotte Grandison, having been disposed to accept the advances of Captain Anderson, is gradually disabused by watching the man emerge through his letters: "When he came to write, my judgment was even still more engaged in his favour than before. But when he thought himself on safe footing with me, he then lost his handwriting, and his style, and even his orthography. I blushed to say it, and I then blushed to see it." (1754, II, Letter XXIX) There is a certain priggishness perhaps in this, but what Richardson is really after in epistolary terms is not a classical elegance or conscious adornment—in fact he satirizes these in Brand's letters in *Clarissa*—but an unaffected naturalness of style, mid-way between the performances of Brand and the semi-literate Jackey in *Pamela*.

Literary values thus figure strongly in Richardson's novels, and he is able to make extensive use of epistolary assumptions in the treatment of character. Pamela's qualifications for her role as commentator, as it develops through the novel, are far from being those of an untutored and illiterate virtue; her improvement gained from her own experiences, and her ability to influence the lives of others, originates from a development at once intellectual and moral.

Pamela's "itch of scribbling" then, which in sheer bulk tends to strain the credulity—for example she writes six letters on her wedding day, beginning at six a.m.—has a twofold purpose in the moral scheme of the novel: first it brings Pamela herself to public recognition, and secondly it propagates her thoughts as influence. Lady Davers states this plainly enough when she writes to Pamela:

> But I'll tell you what has been a great improvement to you; it is your own writings. . . . So that reading constantly, and thus using yourself to write, and enjoying besides a good memory, everything you heard and read became your own; and not only so, but was improved by passing through (your) more salubrious ducts and vehicles. . . . Really, Pamela, I believe, I, too, shall improve by writing to you . . . for already you have made us a family of writers and readers; so that Lord Davers himself is become enamoured of your letters, and desires of all things he may hear read every one that passes between us. (II, 34–35)

The person is quite consciously submerged under her writings and what takes place is significant only insofar as it can be turned into epistolary comment.

Pamela's role thus defined is that of the novelist himself: by bringing literary ability and sufficient reflection to bear upon the crude stuff of personal experience, he shapes it as didactic art. At the beginning, Pamela's energies in the literary sense are taken up with appeals of one kind or another (to possible sources of aid, including Providence), and the personal voice, as we have seen, is often a frantic one. But soon the value of experience as an object lesson is learnt, and Pamela develops a keener critical sense, enlarging the particular to the level of the instructive and general. Thus, after her marriage, she views her earlier unhappy experiences as part of some providential scheme fitting her for a special role: "Great and good God as thou hast enlarged my opportunities, enlarge also my will, and make me delight in dispensing to others a portion of that happiness which I have myself so plentifully received at the hands of thy gracious Providence! Then shall I not be useless in my generation!" (I, 333) Such "enlargement" is a conscious process throughout, and Richardson is careful to emphasize the connexion between Pamela's emergence from obscurity and her formation of a consequential style (see *Selected Letters,* p. 250).

All this accounts for the peculiar shape of the novel. The endless résumées of Pamela's past, the enormous concern with education and the discussions about the art of writing, all of which take up a large part of the novel and which seem to stifle the lively action of the early parts, in fact have a direct bearing on what has gone before, and indeed are its sole justification in the Richardsonian scheme. Briefly stated, his purpose is to render significant what is privately experienced, and to do this by a literate self-awareness expressed and refined through the epistolary form.

Here one can see that Richardson's strength and weakness as a novelist spring from the same source. On the one hand, he narrows the gap between art and life by allowing his characters to create their own literature but, on the other, he widens it again by intruding as commentator regardless of dramatic context. The conscious deliberation that develops in Pamela's writings, as we have seen, is that of the artist himself seeking to objectify the emotional content of experience, and to interpret what goes on below the surface in a series of unambiguous moral statements. Richardson, however, pays the price of the epistolary technique in this: he asks the reader to accept Pamela as both participant and commentator. The result is scarcely successful, and Pamela, convincing enough as sensory sounding-board in the earlier part, is much less convincing as an external commentator later on: the two voices are never successfully fused.

The epistolary technique therefore presented the inexperienced novelist with some knotty problems. Some of these Richardson never properly solved; others he did, including the question of authorial commentary. When he wrote *Clarissa,* he had learnt the value of having several commentaries, and no one character is burdened to the same extent as in *Pamela.* Yet, despite its technical crudities, Richardson's first novel represents a brave attempt to harmonize the two worlds of fiction: the internal and the external narrative viewpoint. He goes further than Fielding does in acquainting the reader both with the reality of the situation and its moral implications and, on the whole, his attempt to intellectualize, in effect from the nervous centre itself, is much more impressive than Fielding's preservation of a conscious externality. Thus, despite its stringent moral tones, *Pamela* remains of compelling interest as a complex work of fiction, but only by stripping away its aura as a *cause célèbre* for the moral satirists will we be able to get to grips with the thing itself.

Pamela's Clothes

by Carey McIntosh

"I will take care of you all, my good Maidens," says Mr. B., as recounted in the opening letter of Richardson's novel; "and for you, *Pamela,* for my dear Mother's sake, I will be a Friend to you, and you shall take care of my Linen." [1] By annexing Pamela to help with his wardrobe, Mr. B. rewards her for past fidelity, and, at the same time, initiates a considerable series of allusions to clothing in *Pamela,* allusions which constitute a unifying leitmotif in Part I of the novel and yoke together a number of otherwise unrelated incidents and themes.

Mr. B.'s first gift to Pamela is a generous assortment of his deceased mother's wearing apparel. In Letter VI, when Pamela records her receipt of "a Suit of my late Lady's Cloaths, and half a Dozen of her Shifts, and Six fine Handkerchiefs, and Three of her Cambrick Aprons, and Four Holland ones," she also registers her opinion that "the Cloaths are fine Silk, and too rich and too good for me, to be sure." [2] Pamela has apparently not yet anticipated her own elevation to a rank commensurate with such costly garments, but she accepts them gratefully, conscious of the disparity between their elegance and her simplicity.

Clothes in *Pamela* function first of all as the visible emblem of social standing. The circumstantiality in Pamela's various lists of various pieces of apparel is entirely appropriate to her self-consciousness about her social position (as well as to her femininity). As formal notice of her resolution not to proceed along the particular avenue of social advancement Mr. B. initially intends for her, she sews for herself a homely rural outfit, a "Dress that will become my Condition," of "good sad-colour'd Stuff" homespun by the local farmer's wife, calico, flannel, and "some pretty good *Scots* Cloth." She pictures to herself the "tawdry

"Pamela's Clothes" by Carey McIntosh. From English Literary History, *Vol. 35, No. 1 (March, 1968), 75–83. Copyright © 1968 by the Johns Hopkins Press. Reprinted by permission of the Johns Hopkins Press.*

[1] Samuel Richardson, *Pamela, or Virtue Rewarded* (Shakespeare Head Press, Oxford, 1929), 4 vols., I, 2. All references to Richardson's novels will be to this edition, by volume and page. Note that in this context "Linen" often meant "undergarments" (OED, def. 3).

[2] I, 11.

Figure" she would make at home in her lady's cast-off silken petticoats,
and decides to reclothe herself in a costume which "Goody *Andrews*'s
Daughter" need not be ashamed of and can put to use when milking
neighbors' cows on cold mornings; nor does she omit appropriate
rustic ornament, "two pretty enough round-ear'd Caps," "two Pair of
ordinary blue Worsted Hose, that make a smartish Appearance, with
white Clocks, I'll assure you!" (Pamela's shrewdness and realistic outlook express themselves even here, in the qualifiers she attaches to her
list of finery, "pretty enough," "smartish.") [3]

To this thrust Mr. B. opposes a suitable riposte, in Letter XXVII,
by sending for Pamela "when nobody else was in the Parlour with
him" and showing off the new "rich Suit of Cloaths" he has brought
home from London in readiness for the next Birth-day at court: "His
Waistcoat stood on End with Gold Lace, and he look'd very grand."
After he has vented his wit on her, Pamela wistfully, tearfully asks "if
this becomes your fine Cloaths, and a Master's Station?" [4] "Fine
clothes" in her mind are so nearly equivalent to "a master's station" as
to make this compound direct object almost a tautology.

In Letter XXIX, shortly before the abduction, when Pamela is
counting on a prompt reunion with her parents, she sorts her clothes
into three bundles, in the presence of Mrs. Jervis (and of course the
lurking Mr. B.): the first parcel contains what her Lady gave her, the
legitimate fruits of service; the second is made up of Mr. B.'s gifts
("they were to be the Price of my Shame"); and finally "poor *Pamela*'s
Bundle, and a little one it is, to the others," "the Companion of my
Poverty, and the Witness of my Honesty." The object of this little
pantomime is to demonstrate her resolution to return to her parents
uncontaminated by "Riches and Pomp" in any form.[5] In fact Pamela
does not succeed in leaving the expensive clothes behind, any more
than she succeeds in resigning her attraction to high life and Mr. B.;
the two larger bundles follow her to Lincolnshire, and the costly
garments they contain become pawns in the struggle between her and
Mrs. Jewkes.[6] When Mr. B. in a huff sends Pamela back to her parents,
the said bundles accompany her on the coach;[7] consequently they return with her to the final reconciliation and are available as the source
of finery more suitable to her new dignity as Mr. B.'s fiancee.[8]

What to wear in her affianced condition is a question of some
delicacy and importance to Pamela:

[3] I, 50 and 49. See I, 70 for Mr. B.'s dexterous manipulation of the message this
costume conveys with regard to social rank, as a pretext for snatching a kiss.
[4] I, 86, 88.
[5] I, 100–103.
[6] I, 159, 176, 247.
[7] II, 5.
[8] II, 83–85, 103.

So I'll get ready. But I won't, I think, change my Garb. Should I do it. it would look as if I would be nearer on a Level with him: And yet, should I not, it may be thought a Disgrace to him? but I will, I think, open the Portmanteau, and, for the first time, since I came hither, put on my best Silk Night-gown. But then, that will be making myself a sort of Right to the Cloaths I had renounc'd; and I am not quite sure I shall have no other Crosses to encounter. So I will go as I am; for tho' ordinary, I am as clean as a Penny, tho' I say it. So I'll e'en go as I am, except he orders otherwise.[9]

Mrs. Jewkes casts several votes for finery, but Mr. B. approves of the milk-maid outfit,[10] and later commands her to wear it for the first encounter with the local gentry of Lincolnshire, as sartorial acknowledgment of her lower-class origins and to remind them (and her) of her "story."[11] In effect Pamela plays the whole central part of the drama in costume,[12] in the rustic grab so carefully described in Letter XX of Volume I, homespun and calico and round-eared cap; it is not until five days before her marriage that her Master requests that she "begin to dress as you use to do,"[13] i.e., as the personal servant of a wealthy member of the country gentry. *After* the wedding, which is private and so calls for only a modest gown of white satin,[14] after her easy triumph over the neighbours, when she has despite bitter resistance conquered Lady Davers, *then* "we must have new Cloaths"[15] and new liveries[16] and diamonds and laces and silks.[17] Much of the last part of Part I is devoted to general celebration, "sharing the loot," which includes not only Pamela's reinvestiture but also fresh drapery for her father, borrowed, at least on the first occasion, from Mr. B.[18]

The second major symbolic role which clothes play in *Pamela* is of course sexual. Mr. B., having honored Pamela with some of his mother's belongings in Letter VI, supplements them in Letter VII with fine stockings and "rich Stays"; and his point comes across:

I was quite astonished, and unable to speak for a while; but yet I was inwardly ashamed to take the Stockens; for Mrs. *Jervis* was not there: If she had, it would have been nothing. I believe I recciv'd them very aukwardly; for he smil'd at my Aukwardness, and said, Don't blush,

[9] II, 24. For further anxiety over suitable clothes, see II, 2, 31, 42.
[10] II, 24, 25, 58.
[11] II, 42, 61.
[12] Intentionally: "I had all this Time worn my own bought Cloaths, tho' my Master would have had it otherwise often" (II, 2).
[13] II, 83.
[14] II, 140.
[15] II, 266.
[16] II, 311, 345.
[17] II, 319–22, 345.
[18] II, 98–100. Pamela is conscious that all her best clothes are borrowed from Mr. B., too (II, 132).

Pamela: Dost think I don't know pretty Maids wear Shoes and Stockens? [19]

For what Mr. B. wishes to say here, clothes are language enough to raise a blush. Pamela's sensitivity to the nuances of costume permits her to notice clothes even in a sexual emergency: she is just going to look into the closet, "slip-shod, when, O dreadful! out rushed my Master, in a rich Silk and Silver Morning Gown." [20] In *Pamela* Part I as a whole there is a good deal of disrobing, most of which we watch like peeping-toms.[21] Mr. B. tells his friends that the beauties of Pamela's person "first attracted my Admiration, and made me her *Lover:* But they were the Beauties of her Mind, that made me her *Husband"*; presumably it is when he is poised half-way between these two roles, sexual and social, that he threatens to undress Pamela in search of her letters.[22] After the wedding, with appreciation, "He was pleased to take Notice of my *Dress;* and, spanning my Waist with his Hands, said What a sweet Shape is here!" [23]

Almost every crucial event in *Pamela* is accompanied either by dressing or by undressing. Strong feelings are expressed, and major actions performed, by means of wearing apparel. As the term of Pamela's servitude in Bedfordshire is prolonged by the embroidery of a waistcoat for Mr. B.,[24] so the security of her emprisonment in Lincolnshire is reinforced by the removal of her shoes.[25] She fakes suicide by tossing an outer-petticoat and cap into the pond.[26] She hides letters for the time being "in her bosom," [27] more permanently "in her under-coat next her linen." [28] It is no more a surprise to find Mr. B. offering "Four complete Suits of rich Cloaths," as well as "Two Diamond Rings," if she will be his mistress, than it is to read that Pamela prefers "the Rags" of poverty[29] to such wicked splendor, and vows that "to lose the best Jewel, my Virtue, would be poorly

[19] I, 13.

[20] I, 79.

[21] I, 75, 241, 247, 254 (Pamela won't undress for bed for fear of Mr. B.), 265, 266, 267, 273, 276, 277, 301 (Pamela tries to dress to protect herself from Mr. B.), 322; II, 85, 99 (Mr. B. here rather coy over men dressing and undressing in general), 140, 183, 243, 246.

[22] II, 228; I, 319–21. Her letters, of course, are the primary medium by which Pamela conveys to Mr. B. "the Beauties of her Mind" (the only case I know in early fiction where the novel [Pamela's letters] becomes an active agent in the novel [*Pamela*]).

[23] II, 186 (my italics).

[24] I, 17, 18, 43, 48, 53, 54, 55, 104.

[25] I, 151, 168, 246.

[26] I, 228, 230–231.

[27] I, 3, 28, 170, 174, 182, 306, 333.

[28] I, 174, 311, 326.

[29] I, 7, 45, 102, 103, 259.

recompens'd by those you propose to give me." [30] The first of numerous injunctions issued to Pamela the bride pertains to "carelessness" in dress "in marry'd Folks," [31] and the first crisis of her marriage, the surprise attack by her husband's sister, is aggravated by the gentility of Pamela's costume—to Lady Davers, an insult; to Pamela, a duty.[32]

*   *   *

The peculiar aptness of this symbolic leitmotif in *Pamela* is a consequence of intrinsic and functional relationships between clothing and, on the one hand, sex, on the other, social position. On some occasions we take clothes off with special relish; for others we put them on with special care.[33] These facts are worth laboring because it is not always recognised that the nature of any symbolism depends not only on its aesthetic organisation but also on the intrinsic qualities of the object chosen to carry symbolic weight.[34] One cannot expect commonplace artifacts like clothes to have high metaphysical meanings, except in a religious context.[35]

On the other hand, the ubiquity and significance of various garments in *Pamela,* in combination with the sensational role they play in the attack on Pamela's chastity, give them a generalised intensity of interest[36] different in kind from our concern for more obviously labeled

[30] I, 259. If Jewels have no extra significance in this context than as exceptionally valuable and portable clothes, Pamela has here made even her Virtue into a kind of garment. It is associations of this sort that Fielding is mocking when he has Shamela reject the money her "person" can earn in favour of the "fortune" she will make by her "virtue." Fielding's burlesque makes special fun of *Pamela's* clothes: see Letters I, VI, VII, X, XII, and the last (unnumbered) letter by Shamela.

[31] II, 177.

[32] II, 196, 204, 213.

[33] Of course clothing metaphors make reference often to areas of experience unrelated to sex or social position. Their contexts may include ornament in general ("proud-pied April, dress'd in all his trim"), protection in general (Clarissa, escaped, wishes to "wrap" herself "in her own Innocence"), and even "customary behavior" (the word *habit* means both "dress" and "accustomed action," in Johnson's Dictionary as well as the OED).

[34] See "The Two Meanings of Symbolism: A Grammatical Exercise," in *Hateful Contraries,* William K. Wimsatt, Jr. (U. of Kentucky Press, 1965), pp. 58–67.

[35] Swift, in *A Tale of a Tub,* exploits for satirical purposes the disparity between traditional religious meanings of the seamless robe of Christianity and the absurdities to which even symbolic robes can be subjected in the name of high fashion and low vanity.

[36] *Pamela's* critics not infrequently single out passages concerned with Pamela's clothes for special notice, often as examples of Richardson's "minuteness" or use of detail: e.g., *Critical Remarks on Sir Charles Grandison, Clarissa, & Pamela* (1754) (Augustan Reprint Society Publication No. 21, Los Angeles, 1950), p. 22; Hazlitt, "Lectures on the English Comic Writers," in *Works,* ed. P. P. Howe, 21 vols., VI (London, 1931), pp. 118–19; Austin Dobson, *Samuel Richardson* (New York and London, 1902), p. 37; David Daiches, *Literary Essays* (London, 1956), pp. 38–9;

symbolic objects like Sophia's muff. That muff is commonplace enough, but it is, unlike Pamela's clothes, a unique object, and by its fourth appearance (*Tom Jones,* X, vi) has entirely stopped warming hands and given itself over to the communication of a specific message of fidelity, affection, and reproach. It calls attention to its own meaningfulness—so do other symbolic objects in eighteenth-century fiction, Robinson Crusoe's husks of corn, and Yorick's caged starling, which speaks not only literally ("I can't get out—I can't get out") but also figuratively, of French tyranny, of British liberty. By contrast, clothing plays so natural and normal a role in *Pamela,* it has so little meaning apart from what adheres to the event it is part of, that it might better be thought of as "leitmotif" than as symbol.

E. M. Forster discusses innocent patterns of allusion like this as "rhythm." Badly done, he feels, rhythm "hardens into a symbol." [37] The distinction is however hard to maintain, in practice as well as in theory: the unobtrusive artifice with which Forster in *Howard's End* manipulates wisps and fields of hay cannot wholly divest them of symbolic overtones. It is precisely this artifice that Pamela's clothes lack. Figurative patterns can, however, be exploited even more unobtrusively, as in the commercial metaphors which govern the language of ordinary statement in Jane Austen.[38] What distinguishes the behavior of clothing in *Pamela* from similar imagery elsewhere, and from ordinary clothes-consciousness,[39] is its eloquence as a series of signs and its functional potency in the plot or action of the novel.

We can gain further perspective on the problem at issue by looking at what wearing apparel does in Richardson's other novels. In general, it seems to loom large only when he is dealing with sex or social class; hence it is far more important in *Clarissa* than in *Grandison,* but in neither book does it occupy center stage as it seems to in *Pamela.* Clarissa's clothes are the outworks of the defense of her virtue. She vexes Lovelace by being "dressed for the day, before she appears even to her servant," [40] and when, by manufacturing a terrific commotion about a pre-arranged fire, he catches her more than half-undressed, she

---

A. D. McKillop, *The Early Masters of English Fiction* (Lawrence, Kansas, 1956), pp. 59 and 60; Douglas Brooks, "Richardson's *Pamela* and Fielding's *Joseph Andrews,*" *Essays in Criticism,* XVII (1967), pp. 159–60; Ian Watt, *The Rise of the Novel* (Berkeley, 1957), pp. 153, 162.

[37] *Aspects of the Novel* (New York, 1927), p. 239. E. K. Brown in *Rhythm in the Novel* (U. of Toronto, 1950), pp. 46–51, expands and illustrates Forster's remarks usefully.

[38] Mark Schorer, "Fiction and the 'Analogical Matrix,'" *Kenyon Review* XI (1949), pp. 540–44.

[39] Natural, in fact almost inevitable, in stories about girls: e.g., *Moll Flanders,* pp. 7, 9, 13, 14, 24, 121 (Everyman Library ed.); *Evelina* (Norton Library, 1965), pp. 15, 16, 17, 18, 27.

[40] IV, 46.

is hard-pressed indeed, in the most erotic-pathetic scene in the novel.[41] Once raped, she refuses to take off her clothes again in Mrs. Sinclair's house, nor will she disrobe during her stay at the house of detention.[42]

Garments of various kinds play more than a casual role in the plot of *Clarissa,* and in Lovelace's plots. When our well-bred heroine has been lured outside the walls of her father's estate, she is embarrassed by her lack of suitable clothes, and humiliated by the protracted negotiations she must engage in to retrieve them.[43] Having escaped from the brothel, she sells her clothes to get money to subsist, and later to pay the doctor, an act which badly hurts her family's pride when they are informed of it.[44] One of the most interesting of Lovelace's talents is his skill in disguise: he is by his own boast a "master of metamorphoses," [45] and doles out costumes to his servants also, to implement more complicated intrigues.[46] Here, clothes are the instrument of Lovelace's deceitfulness and fraudulence (but the acrobatics they perform have a melodramatic cast; the false surfaces presented to Clarissa are merely false, and there is no meaningful depth behind them as there is behind the various costumes in *Pamela*).

Clothes in *Clarissa* are both more diversified and more conventional than in the earlier novel, used as they generally are for the expression and evaluation of character. Thus, Clarissa is distinguished by effortless sartorial elegance; she sets the fashion unawares.[47] Lovelace dresses very well when not in disguise, and is hypersensitive to what outward garb can do for a man, or a woman.[48] Fops and whores overdress, but their deshabille is proportionately slovenly and disgusting.[49] Hickman, though not technically a fop, is "as starched as his Ruffles," and very conservatively outfitted.[50] Clarissa's portrait is drawn formally by Belford on two occasions; she is dressed in "virgin white" for both, under arrest and on her death-bed. The drapery of both pictures, which fall into roughly the same category of figure as Yorick's caged starling, is emblematic not symbolic; it helps to register with the reader Clarissa's new identity as martyr not belle.[51]

In each of these instances, clothing gives us a reliable signal for a moral evaluation which is frequently but not necessarily related to

---

[41] IV, 389 ff.
[42] V, 357, VI, 278.
[43] III, 4, 8, 9, 17, 19, 43, 46, 51, 52, 57, 62, 99, 125, 258, 282–3, 290, 306, 382.
[44] VI, 334, 437, VIII, 129.
[45] III, 52, 154, 333, V, 74.
[46] IV, 270, 299; V, 298, 307; VI, 9.
[47] IV, 78; VII, 101; VIII, 218, 228, 229.
[48] I, 277; III, 27–8, 159; VI, 394–5, 452.
[49] III, 367; IV, 47; VIII, 286, 55–6.
[50] VI, 357, 358.
[51] VI, 298; VII, 449 50. An emblem is of course a conventional, static, and arbitrary kind of symbol often rooted in an ideology of some sort.

social class. It does pretty much the same in *The History of Sir Charles
Grandison*: neither Harriet nor any one else here reaches even the
initial stages of the protracted striptease of the first few hundred pages
of *Pamela*; no one loses caste like Clarissa or gains it like Pamela. Miss
Byron thrusts one trembling toe into the swirling currents of fashionable fun in London—a masquerade ball!—and blushes forever after;
it is her costume as "Arcadian Princess" ("A kind of waistcoat of blue
satten trimmed with silver Point d'Espagne, the skirts edged with silver
fringe," designed to compliment her "shape") which subsequently
reminds her of the frivolity of the affair, since it is all she has of her
own to wear while recuperating at the house of her rescuer.[52] Apart
from this incident, clothes don't do anything in *Grandison*. Sir Charles
dresses richly but not gaudily;[53] Harriet's wedding dress is self-con-
sciously simple ("We want not glare: We are *known* to be able to
afford rich dresses").[54] All this is quite "normal," but it helps us to
recognise both the startling originality of *Pamela* and the important
differences between "Pamela's daughters," of whom Harriet Byron is
one, and Pamela herself. They have in most cases already arrived,
socially, and have been unsexed, so that clothes cannot mean as much
to them as to Pamela.[55]

The first part of *Pamela* was written quickly, without the benefit
of careful revision, and in 1739 Richardson had no established body
of generic conventions or models to guide him towards the "novel."
Pamela is in this respect more naïve ("unsophisticated," "artless,"
even "primitive") than any but a very few other literary productions
of the last three hundred years. A probable consequence of naïveté in
this sense is aesthetic clumsiness, of which *Pamela* has been frequently
accused: A. D. McKillop notices its "crudity," and calls it "a lucky
hit."[56] The indictment is just, but it does not close the case: compared
to *Clarissa*, *Pamela* is ungainly; compared to *Lindamira* (1702) or
Luck at Last (1723), it is adroit and compelling. The elegant manner
in which various narrative and thematic aspects of *Pamela* are linked
by means of clothes, then, constitutes a good example of formal artistry in naïve fiction, and helps to explain why *Pamela* stood out from
the crowd in 1740, why it is read with intense interest today.

[52] I, 172–3, 199, 200, 203, 255.
[53] I, 278, 352–3.
[54] V, 295.
[55] Clothes were at least superficially important in descriptions of the genteel
heroine after 1740 because aside from face, hands, and a fraction of "neck," little
else of her was permitted to be seen. See R. P. Utter and G. B. Needham, *Pamela's
Daughters* (New York, 1936), pp. 49, 158–64, 175.
[56] *Samuel Richardson: Printer and Novelist* (Chapel Hill, 1936), pp. 92, 107. See
also, among many others, Walter Allen, *The English Novel* (London, 1954), p. 43.

PART TWO

View Points

Katherine Hornbeak: From "Richardson's *Familiar Letters* and the Domestic Conduct Books"

If we wish to orient Richardson's work, if we wish to make a genetic study of the letter-writer and the novels, we must approach them by way of the books which were most widespread among the middle class, the social stratum to which Richardson and his readers belonged. As a result of a very strict interpretation of I Timothy 4:7, "But refuse profane and old wives' fables, and exercise thyself rather unto godliness," devout dissenters and Anglicans in the sixteenth and seventeenth centuries eschewed fiction and read books of edification. . . . [Jeremy Taylor's *Holy Living and Holy Dying*, Foxe's *Book of Martyrs*, etc.] In these books Richardson and his readers had their roots. Their ideology was coloured by them and by the sermons expounding the relationships these discussed. . . .

Whatever the manner of Richardson's own contact with these domestic handbooks may or may not have been,* he grew up in a milieu saturated with their standards, principles, and shibboleths. . . . To dip into these little treatises on the relationships of husbands and wives, parents and children, betrothed couples, masters and servants illuminates not only Richardson's letter-writer but his novels as well. Over and over in *Pamela*, *Clarissa*, and *Sir Charles Grandison*, which are really expanded tracts on these relationships (the "relative duties" as Richardson calls them), the novelist has just draped with fiction the principles and ideas of these Puritan handbooks [Austin Dobson recognized this identity of purpose when he wrote that *Pamela* could replace *The Practice of Piety*, or *The Whole Duty of Man* (*Samuel Richardson*, London, 1902, p. 33)].

Let one instance suffice at this point. The burning question, whether

---

From "Richardson's Familiar Letters *and the Domestic Conduct Books" by Katherine Hornbeak, in* Smith College Studies in Modern Language, *XIX (January, 1938), 5, 8–9. Reprinted by permission of the author.*

* [Ed. Note: Richardson's familiarity with the domestic conduct books has been confirmed by the investigations of William M. Sale, Jr., who has established the fact that Richardson printed such volumes as Delany's *Fifteen Sermons upon Social Duties* and Defoe's *New Family Instructor*. "With the tracing of this book and other works of Defoe to Richardson's press, speculation about his possible knowledge of Puritan family literature need not remain so highly conjectural" (*Samuel Richardson*, Ithaca, New York: 1950, p. 162).]

mothers should suckle their infants, which absorbed Pamela and Mr. B. and Pamela's parents for twenty-five pages, is considered in many of the domestic conduct books. *Of Domesticall Duties* offers a discussion "of mothers giving sucke to their owne children," buttressed with much Scriptural precedent. *The Whole Duty of Man,* in the reading supplied for Sunday XIV, urges the point. In Jeremy Taylor's life of Jesus he introduces a discourse "of Nursing Children, in imitation of the blessed Virgin Mother." Archbishop Tillotson, in one of his sermons, devotes a section to the issue: "In the tender and careful nursing of Children." Anyone who will look into these arguments will be convinced that Richardson, through Pamela, offers his readers "the best that has been known and thought" on the matter.

Ian Watt: From "The Naming of Characters in Defoe, Richardson, and Fielding"

The novelist—following the convention of comedy noted by Aristotle[1]—usually invents the names, as well as the actions, of his characters. In most fiction until the eighteenth century the names used were quite different from those used in real life; they were "characteristic," artificial and conventional designations suited to the half-generalized types that figure in romance and pastoral. It was only in the later developments of fiction—the professedly nonfictional "true histories," biographies, and memoirs—that the names used could possibly be mistaken for those of real people. . . .

In christening their beloved daughter, John and Elizabeth Andrews disregarded the tradition of piety which was embodied in their own christian names and that of their author. The name 'Pamela' was contained neither in the Bible nor in the Calendar of Saints.

It was also extremely rare in real life. The Richardsonian pronunciation—evidenced in the verses Pamela makes[2]—moved the accepted stress from Paméla to Pámela. Richardson[3] and Fielding[4] both comment on the rarity of the name, and the change of accent occupied

From "The Naming of Characters in Defoe, Richardson, and Fielding" by I. [Ian] P. Watt, in Review of English Studies, *XXV (October, 1949), 322, 325–26, 328–29. Reprinted by permission of the Clarendon Press, Oxford.*

[1] "In comedy . . . the poet first constructs the plot on the lines of probability, and then inserts characteristic names. . . . But tragedians still keep to real [i.e. historical] names" (*Poetics,* trans, Butcher, 9).

[2] Letter XXXI.

[3] "Pamela—did you say?—A queer sort of Name! I've heard of it somewhere! Is it a Christian or a Pagan Name?" [*Pamela* (1st ed., Part II, London, 1741), iii. 316].

[4] ". . . a very strange name, Paméla or Paméla: some pronounced it one way and some the other" (*Joseph Andrews,* Bk. IV, ch. 12).

Aaron Hill, Mrs. Barbauld,[5] and, at much greater length, the pages of *Notes and Queries*.[6]

It has been generally assumed that the name comes from Sidney's *Arcadia*,[7] and a passage from the second part of *Pamela* shows that Richardson assumed both the heroine's and the reader's knowledge of Musidorus as the name of Pamela's lover.[8] We can certainly assume that Richardson knew that his heroine's name suggested "vaine amatorious romance," rather than the pedestrian piety of the Andrews household. The only strictly realistic interpretation of Pamela's name, therefore, is social pretentiousness on the part of the parents—as Fielding[9] was quick to point out by giving Shamela's mother a triple string of fashionable names—Henrietta Maria Honora—which give the lie to her professions of humility.

The more important explanation of this departure from realism is that Richardson, despite his frequent assertions of superiority, continues the tradition of romance, especially in his treatment of women, whose literary interests and personal ideals were still, as he knew, influenced by the patterns of romantic love, even in the matter of names.[10]

. . . *Pamela*, of course, is romance with a difference. The central character is not only Pamela, the arcadian heroine, all simple innocence and artless beauty; she is also the poor Miss Andrews who has her way to make in the world. The love theme is suggested by her christian name, but it is given a realistic setting by a surname which

[5] *Correspondence of Samuel Richardson* (London, 1804), i. lxxviii.

[6] 2d Ser. ix. 305, 394; 5th Ser. x. 88, 234; 9th Ser. xii. 141, 330. . . .

[7] e.g. by Charlotte Yonge, *History of Christian Names* (London, 1863), ii. 485; Paul Dottin, *Samuel Richardson* (Paris, 1931), pp. 59, 72; E. Poetzsche, *Samuel Richardsons Belesenheit* (Kiel, 1904), p. 41.

[8] Pamela relates that at a masquerade "a Presbyterian Parson came up, and bid me look after my Musidorus—so I doubted not by this, it must be one who knew my name to be Pamela" (Pt II, Letter LVI). The *Arcadia* was certainly well known in the period—it was reprinted twice in 1725 and again in 1739. It was admired by several of Richardson's friends, including Sarah Fielding, Mrs. Delany, and Aaron Hill. [See S. Fielding, *Lives of Cleopatra and Octavia*, cit. A. D. McKillop, "The personal Relations between Richardson and Fielding," *M. P.* xxviii (1931), 433; *Autobiography and Correspondence of Mrs. Delany*, ed. S. C. Woolsey (Boston, 1882), p. 258; D. Brewster, *Aaron Hill* (New York, 1915), p. 190.] Further strong evidence is contained in W. M. Sale's forthcoming study of Richardson's printing-house, where, mainly by comparing types and ornaments, it is established that Richardson printed at least a part of the *Arcadia* as his share of the 1724/5 edition of Sidney's works.

[9] The attribution of *Shamela* to Fielding is discussed, and further strengthened, by C. B. Woods in his article "Fielding and the Authorship of *Shamela*," *P. Q.* xxxv (1946), 248–72.

[10] Dottin writes that in *Pamela* and *Clarissa*, Richardson used names "suffisamment romanesques pour impressionner le genre de lecteur qu'il s'agissait d'atteindre" (op. cit., p. 72).

involves her in the world of family, material, and religious obligations. The conflict of the two roles—Pamela against Miss Andrews—is
the essence of the novel; and thereby Richardson initiates the new
development of fiction in the eighteenth century, which sets the romantic or aspirational side of personality against a realistically presented background of domestic environment and external necessity. . . .

Richardson has endowed his heroine more richly than Mr. B. for
this struggle. It is difficult to attribute a full and complex personality
to a mere cipher, and, consequently, he remains a lay figure in a
"secret history," with no more reality in the novel than he had originally as the subject of a piece of whispered gossip about the local
squire. . . .

There were, no doubt, several "obvious reasons" why Richardson
did not invent a name for Mr. B., although he had invented a full
one for his heroine. He could justify himself by the strong tradition
against naming the nobility and gentry in writing,[11] and it is probable
that he wished to turn the convention to account by retaining, whether
justified or not, the suggestive and saleable aura of a true scandal of
high life. Dr. Johnson—no credulous reader—thought that "a writer
does not feign a name of which he only gives the initial letter," [12] and
Richardson certainly wished to give such an impression. But there
are other reasons why Mr. B. remains a cipher. Richardson's interest
was focused upon the heroine, and any increase in the reality of her
antagonist would have undermined the credibility of her interpretation of the story; a more convincing Mr. B., validated by a complete
name, would have revealed the fact that names, and lack of names,
are a part of the legerdemain which allows Pamela her triumph.

[11] See H. T. Buckle, *History of Civilisation in England* (London, 1858), i. 238, fn.
[12] *Lives of the English Poets*, ed. G. B. Hill (Oxford, 1905), iii. 381.

Leslie A. Fiedler: From *Love and Death in the American Novel*

The novel proper could not be launched until some author imagined a prose narrative in which the Seducer and Pure Maiden were
brought face to face in a ritual combat designed to end in marriage or
death; the form and its mythology were born together, in the works
of Samuel Richardson, a melancholy and pious printer, who in 1740
became the first modern novelist almost by mistake. He wrote three

From Love and Death in the American Novel *by Leslie A. Fiedler, pp. 29, 31, 42.
Copyright © 1966 by Leslie A. Fiedler. Reprinted by permission of Stein and Day,
Inc., and Jonathan Cape, Ltd.*

large, tearful novels before he was through, *Pamela, Clarissa,* and *Sir Charles Grandison*—the first still read, at least in schools, but condescendingly (did not Fielding laugh it from the scene with *Shamela* and *Joseph Andrews?*), the other two now left to gather dust in libraries, though all Europe once wept over *Clarissa*; and Jane Austen, who could not bear the tragic tone of the greater work, learned her craft from *Grandison. Autres temps, autres moeurs.*

Pamela is the comedy of sentimental love, *Clarissa* the tragedy; *Grandison* is an afterword that added little new. . . .

Practically everyone who knows the name of Richardson knows the meager plot of *Pamela*: how the virtuous governess resists the advances of her employer's son and finally compels him to marry her. It is the first success story of the female bourgeois world, at once practical, prurient, and edifying—a thoroughgoing piece of *almost* unconscious duplicity, though quite charming all the same. The "almost" is the secret of Richardson's deepest appeal: he knows really what Pamela is after all along, knows her for the female Ben Franklin that she is, though he does not quite know he knows it; this happy state of quasi-insight (he never falsifies the hidden motivations of his protagonists) he shares with his heroines and the readers who identify with them. . . .

To one brought up inside the view of the English novel that was universally accepted at the beginning of the present century, Richardson is hard to appreciate. Was his reputation not almost immediately deflated by the irony of Fielding? Did not readers move with relief from the fetid atmosphere of his airless boudoirs to the broad open-air vistas of the pseudo-Shakespearean novel of masculine protest? Did not ingenious plotting and fast action, good theater, replace the tedious revelation of the dark underside of the souls of young girls? Of course they did not; for the novel must continue to carry the torch to the back of the cave (whatever else it does in addition) or surrender its birthright, its essential function. Parody destroys nothing; it is only a reluctant and shamefaced way of honoring an example one is ashamed to acknowledge, and, for one too proud to attempt so popular a form as the novel without tongue in cheek, a way of becoming a novelist.

For a long time, however, the Fielding–Scott–Dickens fanciers controlled criticism of the novel in England, defending their preferred authors, in more genteel times, as "cleaner" than Richardson and his school and in less genteel days, as more "vigorous." Always they depreciated the strain that passes from Richardson to Jane Austen to George Eliot to Henry James as somehow too feminine and inward to be truly Anglo-Saxon. Nonetheless, even in Scott and Dickens, the tradition of the sentimental novel survived. . . .

George Sherburn: From "Samuel Richardson's Novels
and the Theatre: A Theory Sketched"

When Pope wrote

> Our wives read Milton and our daughters plays,

he was being too complimentary to the wives; for both wives and
daughters—and in many cases the paterfamilias himself—read plays.
Among these male readers Samuel Richardson may seem to have been
one. There is little evidence as to his play-going habits, but his friend-
ships with Colley Cibber, Aaron Hill, and even Edward Young, as
well as his interest in stage morals as seen in *The Apprentice's Vade
Mecum* (1733) and in his *Seasonable Examination of the Pleas and
Pretensions of, and Subscribers to, Play-Houses, Erected in Defiance
of the Royal Licence* (1735), make an interest in the theatre and in
plays more than probable. In a letter to Mrs. Watts (May 13, 1756),
as Professor Duncan Eaves informs the writer, Richardson regrets that
ill health keeps him away from the theatre as well as from hearing the
debates in Parliament. "The rational amusement of a good play,"
he says, had been (presumably in days before *Pamela*) "a favourite
diversion."

The influence of the drama on Richardson's novels seems to have
been neglected. He got behavioral instruction from courtesy books
and books of family instruction; he got the names of persons and
(perhaps more important) his use of the dialectic of love, which he
habitually detailed in long conversations, from French romances of
the seventeenth century; but he got a diversity of techniques and
materials from his knowledge of plays.

For the English he revolutionized the novel by his strong focus on
central plot-situation (as opposed to the loose episodic picaresque tradition, or of biography, or even of the epic tradition supported by
Fielding), and by a hitherto unparalleled employment of conversation.
At times his "dialogues" last for almost a hundred pages, and habitually they are long. His chief indebtedness to the theatre would be plot-
focus, character types, and vivid, extensive conversation.

. . . Both in *Pamela I* and in *Clarissa* there is a concentration of
attention on a single situation, a concentration that is dramatic in
origin, rather than a diffused awareness of successive episodes such as
earlier narratives used. *Pamela II* and *Sir Charles Grandison* have less

*From "Samuel Richardson's Novels and the Theatre: A Theory Sketched" by
George Sherburn, in* Philological Quarterly, *XLI (January, 1962), 325, 326, 328–29.
Copyright © 1962, by The University of Iowa. Reprinted by permission of John E.
Simmons, Director of Publications.*

focus, are more episodic, and owe far more to courtesy books than to the theatre. . . .

The earliest of the notable "big scenes" that Richardson invented is that between Pamela and Lady Davers, which is easily the most brilliant bit in *Pamela,* and which must have been to the author a revelation of power. Among the tense but not tragic scenes it is perhaps Richardson at his very best. The famous pen-knife scene in Clarissa has often been praised: it approaches operatic heights—rising in its tragic suspense above mere drama. Of these dramatic scenes, composed almost certainly with the theatre in mind, any reader of these novels will recall many. . . .

At his best, thus, Richardson writes as if present and participating in a scene. "Writing to the moment" became his trump trick. One need not depend upon the theatre for that, but one may (and Richardson did) possess the gift, and a knowledge of the theatre might help.

Albert M. Lyles: "Pamela's Trials"

One of the few realistic details in Richardson's characterization of *Pamela's* Mr. B. is that he is a justice of the peace. Richardson's use of this detail seems to be a crude device for justifying Pamela's inaction in the face of Mr. B.'s attacks on her chastity, an inaction not sufficiently explained by the master-servant relationship. And in Letter XXV Pamela writes to her parents that although, "I can safely swear the peace against him: . . . , alas! he is greater than any constable: he is a justice himself." [1] However, after Pamela's abduction to Lincolnshire, where Mr. B.'s Bedfordshire justiceship is presumably ineffective, the fact that he is also a Lincolnshire justice and has sworn out a warrant for Pamela's arrest is revealed to her only after she has determined to make no further attempts to escape. Mr. B.'s being a justice then does not function as an excuse for inaction in the crucial Lincolnshire scenes. However, the characterization of Mr. B. as a justice permits Richardson to dramatize climactic scenes of the novel in terms of the legal metaphor of a trial and thus to make more obvious the relationship of both the melodramatic and comic scenes to the theme of virtue rewarded.

Although the metaphor of a trial is employed several times early in the novel, notably when Pamela is threatened with expulsion from

From "Pamela's Trials" by Albert M. Lyles, in College Language Association Journal, *VIII (March, 1965), 290–92. Reprinted by permission of Therman B. O'Daniel, Editor.*

[1] All quotations from the novel come from the Norton Library edition.

the Bedfordshire estate after Mr. B.'s approaches to her in his mother's chamber, the climactic, intense use of it occurs when Mr. B. returns to Lincolnshire. After taking a deposition from Mrs. Jewkes for two and a half hours, he summons Pamela to his presence. Richardson describes the scene as a trial. There Pamela discovers that although she pleads for mercy and attempts to accuse Mrs. Jewkes, she is herself on trial. She is charged with tempting Mr. Williams to "undo himself," slandering her fellow servants, and obstinately disobeying her master. Pamela sees the uselessness of appeals and compares herself to the lamb "tried before the vulture, on the accusation of the wolf," an interesting anticipation of Justice Buzzard in *Joseph Andrews*. Despite the presence of Mrs. Jewkes, in this trial Mr. B. is prosecutor as well as judge. As prosecutor he is tempted to forgive, an anticipation of the later scene when preparing to read Pamela's letters, he tells her: "You have too powerful a pleader within me." Yet as judge he finds Pamela guilty: "Your doom is fixed," the judgment to be sexual violation, although he will still attempt to gain her consent to be his "vile kept mistress."

Within Mr. B.'s court Pamela has been found guilty, and of Prosecutor B.'s charges, although one could question their seriousness, she is guilty. But Pamela is aware that at the same time she is being tried in another court by another judge, the heavenly one by God, and here she is convinced of her innocence. From the earthly judge, whom she has seen to be a "very bad judge," she cannot expect mercy or even justice. Her justice must come from God, Who knows her innocence and Who, she is confident early in the novel, will save her from Mr. B.'s attacks. Later after she has resigned herself to God's Providence, symbolized by her refusal to drown herself, and when Mr. B., his patience exhausted, has come to Lincolnshire to rape her, she despairingly cries to Mrs. Jewkes of an ultimate divine justice: "though I can have neither justice or mercy here, and cannot be heard in my defence, yet a time will come, may be, when I *shall* be heard, and when your own guilt will strike you dumb." [2] At this point, found guilty by the perverted form of the earthly court, Pamela anticipates what is more important for her than rape or death, a judgment-day vindication.

But, although she is unaware of it, another trial, a more realistic one, is underway—the testing of her qualifications as a wife. Her invincible chastity is established unmistakably when the judge is unable to carry out the sentence of sexual violation. Then other only slightly less important qualities are tested. Mr. B.'s demanding to see her eat a boiled chicken wing is an almost ludicrous test of her

[2] The very strong Puritanical and Evangelical flavor of *Pamela* is obvious, but Pamela's comment suggests specifically the Methodist habit, by 1740 already being satirized, of summoning opponents to the Bar of Judgment.

social poise and skill. He discovers that Pamela has all of the qualities
—chastity, good manners, wit, and finally when she returns to Lincolnshire a willingness to repose confidence in him—which he demands of
a wife. And the way is prepared for the collaboration of the earthly
and heavenly judges—virtue is to be rewarded, and Pamela need not
wait for justice in heaven.

The final use of the trial metaphor comes as the climax to the comic
imprisonment of Pamela by Lady Davers. When Pamela recounts her
escape, Sir Simon Darnford, also a justice, comments: "'Twas well
you was a prisoner, or your spouse and I should have sat in judgment
upon you, and condemned you to a fearful punishment for your first
crime of *laesae majistatis.*" This passage suggests that Richardson did
not use the trial metaphor to dramatize the inequities of the English
legal system, as Fielding was to do later, and that he was not even
primarily concerned with the verisimilitude of the trial scenes. But the
metaphor that he had used to reveal the power of Mr. B. and to
dramatize *Pamela*'s theme of virtue rewarded becomes finally a comic
sally, a mark of the dissolving of melodrama into social comedy, and a
link between the disparate halves of the novel.

Owen Jenkins: From "Richardson's *Pamela* and Fielding's 'Vile Forgeries'"

How seriously are we to take Henry Fielding's facetious boast on
the title page of *Shamela* that in his parody "the many notorious fals-
hoods and misrepresentations of a book called *Pamela,* are exposed
and refuted?" A recent tendency among scholars has been to say, in
effect, amen! Thus the latest editor of *Shamela* echoes Fielding and
proclaims that "by the time the burlesque has run its course, the
absurdities and pretensions of *Pamela* have been exposed once and
for all." [1] And in *Pamela-Shamela: A Study of the criticisms, burlesques, parodies, and adaptations of Richardson's "Pamela"* (University of Nebraska Press, 1960), Bernard Kreissman, although observing that Fielding's specific objections are open to criticism (pp.
16–18), is nevertheless so confident that Richardson could not reply
to Fielding and other critics that he puts Richardson's only public
opportunity for a defense of his novel, the continuation of *Pamela,*
"outside the scope of this study," adding only this as his reason: "and

From "Richardson's Pamela *and Fielding's 'Vile Forgeries'" by Owen Jenkins, in*
Philological Quarterly, *XLIV (April, 1965), 200–201, 202–4, 206. Copyright* ©
*1965 by The University of Iowa. Reprinted by permission of John E. Simmons,
Director of Publications.*

[1] Martin C. Battestin, ed., *Joseph Andrews and Shamela* (Boston, 1961), p. xi.

a good thing it is, for two duller volumes have rarely graced the English language" (p. 10).

Such supreme confidence in the impossibility of Richardson's answering Fielding's comic criticism ignores some interesting facts. First of all, many critics persist in thinking *Pamela* is a fascinating novel, perhaps even a very good one. Among these critics we may certainly number Richardson himself, and the question is really not the possibility or impossibility of reply but rather whether Richardson thought he had the ability to answer his critics. Second, we know in fact that Richardson thought himself capable of "strokes of humour, and innocent raillery" when the occasion required.[2] *Shamela* would seem to be such an occasion. Third, we also know as a matter of fact that Richardson set to work on the continuation of *Pamela* less than two weeks after *Shamela* had been published.[3] Fourth, if we would only read the continuation we should discover the fact pointed out long ago by Mrs. Barbauld that the apparent sequel "is less a continuation than the author's defense of himself."[4] . . .

Richardson the moralist certainly thought that the purpose of *Pamela* was the same as that of the *Familiar Letters* he had been writing when the story of Pamela came into his mind. But was it? A comparison of the advice given in the *Letters* to a young girl "in Service, on hearing of her Master's attempting her Virtue," and the apparent lesson of Pamela's conduct in just these circumstances reveals an apparent contradiction. In the *Familiar Letters,* where the title page announced the work would teach readers "how to think and act justly and prudently, in the common concerns of human life," Richardson's advice to the endangered maid is as wise as it is simple: go home![5] In the novel, which proclaimed on its title page a dedication to "the principles of virtue and religion," the advice to young maids in sexual danger is apparently just the opposite: stay, your master may relent and marry you.

How do we reconcile such contradictory advice in two books written to serve the cause of virtue? This is the problem Richardson the moralist faces in the second half of *Pamela:* he must prove Pamela's conduct in the first half of the book morally right although, judged by the probabilities of everyday life, it was morally wrong. His solution is inherent in the artistic requirements of a complex plot, the gradual

---

[2] See Richardson's "Preface" to his *Familiar Letters on Important Occasions* (1741; reprinted with an introduction by Brian W. Downs [London, 1928]).

[3] *Shamela* was published on April 4, 1741. In August, 1741, Richardson wrote James Leake saying that he had begun work on the continuation of *Pamela* "in the middle of last April" (quoted by Alan D. McKillop in *Samuel Richardson* [University of North Carolina Press, 1936], p. 53).

[4] *The Correspondence of Samuel Richardson* (London, 1804), I, lxxvii.

[5] Downs, pp. 164–65.

revelation that the characters of Pamela and Mr. B. are not what they first appear to be. Thus Richardson devotes the second half of the novel to tedious explanations of the motives of the characters in the first half, and to two lively episodes which prove that neither Pamela nor Mr. B. is what we once thought, a half-consciously scheming servant maid and an inept seducer. In the scenes with Mr. B.'s sister, Lady Davers, Pamela is sincere in her defense of what she thinks her station in life requires, and through the capitulation of Lady Davers, a sister who allowing for differences in sex and circumstances is almost an exact duplicate of her brother's temperament, we see that Pamela's virtue will indeed always be rewarded. Similarly, Mr. B., through his disclosure of a previous affair with Miss Sally Godfrey, is revealed to be not the mere seducer he seemed at the beginning of the novel; in fact, the episode with the unfortunate Sally proves that he was, although himself unaware of it, precisely the sort of man to be moved to honorable love by Pamela's virtue.

Once the principal characters have been shown to be distinctly unusual individuals, not types of the servant maid and the libidinous squire, the morality of Pamela's actions in the first half of the novel is justified on the grounds that the predicament was a special case. And all the while Richardson the moralist has been establishing the special circumstances required for judging Pamela's story Richardson the novelist has been emphasizing the probabilities of the first half of the novel, its marvelous and yet convincing turn of events. Thus far the novelist and the moralist have been working in concert, and with the story of Sally Godfrey the novel ends.

Unfortunately for its integrity, however, Richardson the editor once again appears in the final pages of the work, now drawing general morals from a story he has spent the last half of the novel proving to be an exception to any general rules. The editor is trying to persuade us that the art of the novelist can be applied to didactic ends, to convince us that *Pamela* is a conduct book like the *Familiar Letters*. He has either not detected, or has chosen to ignore, the duplicity at the heart of this or any other "wonderful" didactic story: the reader is tricked into drawing universal morals from the experience of characters the author has begun by portraying as types but concluded by revealing to be exceptional individuals. Proving a general rule by an exceptional case is the key to many great moral tales, at least those with a complex plot, and the deception involved is usually unnoticed because the reader is convinced of the general truth of the moral *before* he begins reading and is convinced by the artistry of the teller of the special truth of the story *while* he is reading. That general moral rules have valid exceptions is the tacit premise on which the marvelous didactic tale is based, but when Richardson editorially points the morals at the end of his story he only emphasizes the ambiguities inherent in the peripeties and discoveries of the complex plot, ambiguities essential to the art of the novel but fatal to any profession of the simple, unqualified moral advice necessary in a conduct book designed to teach one "how to act justly and prudently in the common concerns of human life.". . .

An alert reading of the continuation of *Pamela* in light of the circumstances and problems I have described confirms the observation that Richardson, like his principal characters, has a "divided mind," a tendency to "have it both ways" [6] rather than make a clear choice. He consistently keeps up the pretense that *II Pamela* is a sequel whereas in truth its principal concern is a defense of the original novel.[7] Like his hero and heroine, Richardson is a man obsessed; he seems intent on answering each and every criticism of his novel, and as a result such dull topics as the proper rank of Pamela's husband are discussed at great length. This mixture of trivial with fundamental critical questions, of the pretense of narrative with the principal business of defense, makes *II Pamela* tedious reading—unless the reader is as interested in the correct reading of the original novel as its author or in watching the author reply to his critics, and particularly to *Shamela*. If one limits one's concerns in the continuation to these questions, then *II Pamela* may have genuine merit as a work of criticism and considerable wit as a counter-polemic.

[6] The phrases are those of Brian W. Downs, *Richardson* (London, 1928), pp. 128 and 70.
[7] In the "Preface" to the continuation Richardson is significantly vague on his purposes. He says that although he had not intended a sequel he was "provoked into a necessity of altering his intention. But he is willing to decline saying any thing upon so well-known a subject" (II, v).

John Samuel Bullen: From "Time in *Pamela*"

The location of narrative within fixed and specified limits of time, and, further, the employment of time (its duration, its relativity, its apparent absence) in various significant ways in the development of a fictional world—these have become common procedures in the novel since Richardson. On a novel's attention to relationships in time depends the power of probability in its characters and actions; yet a novel's sequence of time draws its significance from actualized elements that are shown to exist within it. . . . Thus, in the full dimension of a novel, time, character, and event are mutually de-

From "Time in Pamela" in Time and Space in the Novels of Samuel Richardson, by John Samuel Bullen (Logan, Utah: Utah State University Press, Monograph Series, XIX [July, 1965]), 7, 8–11. Copyright © 1965 by John Samuel Bullen. Reprinted by permission of the author.

pendent, infusing one another with the particularity that negotiates the novel's realism. . . .

Richardson, however, did not particularize time elements simply as a matter of course, even though the form in which he wrote lends itself so easily to an almost automatic accounting for days and weeks. In *Pamela*, he appears to have learned almost in the process of writing that attention to time gave greater weight to the other details of his novel. The early letters of Pamela to her parents, for example, bear no label of day, time, or place, epistolary elements that are scrupulously attended to through most of the rest of Richardson's work. Nor do Pamela's early letters carry much internal concern with time or with the placement of events in time relationships. In her first letter, Pamela announces the death of her lady, but does not say when the death occurred; by the twentieth letter, we are amazed to learn that fourteen months have elapsed "since my lady's death" (I, 41),[1] for we are still involved in the preliminary stages of B.'s forays against Pamela. Other time relationships are equally vague in the early sections. Pamela reveals in her fourth letter that Lady Davers "has been a month at our house" (I, 6), though nothing else has indicated the passage of this much time in Pamela's own experience. Even events that are crucial to Pamela's situation are located hazily: [O]ne day he came to me, as I was in the summer house" (I, 14). Not "last Wednesday," but "one day." Within certain scenes, which themselves are obscurely placed in time, Pamela's account does begin to suggest the ticking of the clock: "Well, you may believe how uneasily I passed the time until his appointed hour came. Every minute, as it grew nearer, my terrors increased" (I, 27). But not until Pamela is confined at the Lincolnshire estate and begins to keep a journal does she start a methodical calendarizing of her narrative: "I am now come to Monday, the 5th day of my bondage and misery" (I, 125). From this point, in fact, to the end of *Pamela 1*, her communications are dated at least with the weekday of composition, so that the rhythm of the narrative comes to be somewhat governed by the passage of time. The lack, however, of an overall structure of time for the novel tends to isolate the Lincolnshire section as an independent unit.

One could, of course, advance the supposition that Richardson's shift, after the first hundred pages of his novel, from a generalized to a particularized treatment of time was deliberate. It would be difficult, however, to support such a theory by citing advantages that he might consciously have hoped to gain from such a maneuver. It seems more likely that the change resulted from Richardson's recognition

---

[1] In this study, all citations refer to *The Novels of Samuel Richardson*, with a Life of the Author and Introductions by W. L. Phelps. 19 vols. (New York, 1901–02). [The references to *Pamela*, then, are to vol. I of that collection.]

that as Pamela's predicament became increasingly specialized it demanded a more open acknowledgement of the consciousness of time that she would have in the circumstances, and, consequently, required a more tightly controlled time sequence than he had presented in the earlier passages. Whatever the cause, the consequence of the change is apparent, both in the increased vividness of scene and character after Pamela's arrival at the Lincolnshire estate and in the strengthened suggestion of a situation that undergoes complications and reaches its solution over a passage of time.[2] The world of the early sections of *Pamela* is almost as timeless as the world of *The Pilgrim's Progress* or *Euphues*. And in this timeless world, the case of Pamela seems almost as hypothetical as the situations in Richardson's own *Familiar Letters*. It may well be that the change we observe after the first hundred pages of *Pamela* shows the English novel coming to its first struggle with the patterns of experienced time.

If, during the writing of *Pamela I*, Richardson learned the value of closely observed time relationships, he did not immediately apply his lesson to his work, for in *Pamela II* he returns to a timeless world. He creates, in fact, a world in which almost no acknowledgement is made of the calendar or the clock. . . . The fact . . . that *Pamela II* is not regulated by a consistent time system is a contributing cause to its major flaw, the disjunction between narrative and non-narrative elements, a flaw that does not reappear in Richardson's work until *Sir Charles Grandison*. This gap is more noticeable in the sequel than in the original novel, probably because of the relatively thin line of action onto which is basted a disproportionate amount of discursive material. But even in a moderate amount this material would seem gratuitous, for it has no temporal connection with a continuity of events and therefore has no point of reference.

In *Pamela*, then, we see an unsure treatment of time that further reveals the tentative nature of Richardson's narrative powers at this point in his career. We see that the weakness of time in *Pamela* results not so much from an inherent defect in the narrative system itself as from Richardson's own inability to fuse, within the functioning of that system, his disparate attempts to present Pamela as both an individual girl at her moment in time and as a timeless example. More likely, the weakness results from Richardson's failure even to recognize that such a fusion is artistically desirable. Thus, the sections of *Pamela I* that do operate in particularized time seem the accidental results of Richardson's yielding to the demands of his narrative

---

[2] Slightly less than two months pass between Pamela's arrival at the Lincolnshire estate and her marriage to B., but practically every day of the period is accounted for. In contrast, the preceding period, which seems much shorter, apparently covers more than a year. It is impossible, however, to determine the length of time covered by the early period with any accuracy.

method rather than controlling it, a supposition that is further supported by the sole example of situational time in *Pamela II*. To observe a more successful and purposeful handling of time we must turn our attention to *Clarissa*.

Robert Adams Day: From *Told in Letters: Epistolary Fiction before Richardson*

All we know of Richardson's life and character indicates that his knowledge of English novels written in his earlier years must have been sketchy and slight. As an industrious and priggish youth, as a hardworking young printer and a self-made businessman, he would have scorned novels as wasteful of precious time, frivolous, and downright wicked. He might have read fictional pieces with a pious purpose, such as Bunyan's, or with a thick coating of improving morals, such as Defoe's; but mere fiction was probably in very dubious standing for him and his early associates. That he had considerable knowledge of contemporary plays, derived from reading or seeing them in his relatively giddier youth, has been deduced from references in his novels and letters; he read and commented on various novels in his leisurely later years. But plays, bad as their reputation was, occupied a higher position than did novels. Richardson knew the *Tatler* and *Spectator,* but evidence for his early knowledge of fiction is so slight and vague that theorizing on it is purposeless.[1]

We need not suppose that Richardson needed to know earlier fiction in order to write *Pamela*. The accounts we have of his life indicate that writing letters—including very long letters, copies, and letters to persons living under his own roof—was as natural to him as breathing.[2] Letters, for business, pleasure, or art, were a very important part of his life. There is no reason why writing a story in letters should not have seemed both obvious and very congenial to him. . . .

From "Before Richardson, and After" by Robert Adams Day. From Told in Letters: Epistolary Fiction before Richardson *(Ann Arbor: University of Michigan Press, 1966), pp. 206–7, 208–9. Reprinted by permission of the publisher.*

[1] See McKillop, *Samuel Richardson*, pp. 169–89, and his "Supplementary Notes on Richardson as a Printer," *Studies in Bibliography*, XII (1959), 214–18. Pamela mentions Philips' *Distrest Mother* at length; Charles Johnson's play *Caelia* (1733) may have contributed plot material to *Clarissa*; Rowe's *The Fair Penitent* and Otway's *Orphan* are mentioned in it. Richardson referred to *The Princess of Cleves*, but in a manner that makes it uncertain whether he had read it. See *The History of Sir Charles Grandison* (Shakespeare Head edition, 6 vols., Oxford, 1930), VI, 225–26.

[2] See Brian W. Downs, *Richardson* (London, 1928), p. 167.

The form in which *Pamela* was cast seems to have caused little surprise. One reviewer commented:

> The Manner in which we come to the Knowledge of them [the incidents in Pamela's story] is very singular. The Narrative is all of her own relating, in a Series of Letters to her Father and Mother, jointly for the most part, and in a few Instances to the latter alone,[3]

but readers in general apparently found nothing curious in the epistolary presentation of the novel. Richardson did not refer to his technique until later, and the flood of eulogistic criticism which poured in on him after 1740 was at first concerned only with praising the morality and value of the piece.[4] Not until the time of *Clarissa* did he and his correspondents become much interested in the niceties of putting fiction into letters. Certainly, the general reader of 1740 was sufficiently habituated to familiar letters in and out of fiction to find nothing very surprising in the method of *Pamela*.

Richardson and his friends did comment on what they found to be new in *Pamela*—the plain language, the relatively unromantic story, and the moralizing. *Pamela* was something new in fiction, a novel which one need not be ashamed of reading. More importantly, though this was seldom commented on in Richardson's time, *Pamela* carried the technique of "discoursing" to far greater lengths than had any previous piece of original English fiction. Its only parallels in that respect were the novels of Boursault, Marivaux, and Crébillon. The story was of the simplest in plot and action. Earlier writers would have found it suitable for treatment in fifty pages at the most; indeed, a very similar tale (which has been suggested as a source for *Pamela*) was told in a single *Spectator* by John Hughes.[5] But Richardson expanded his story to two and then four volumes. He expanded it not by complicating the plot and introducing new action or (in *Pamela I*) by disgressions not to the purpose, but by making it move with unprecedented slowness, while each tiny step was reflected upon, turned in all directions, and painstakingly examined by Pamela's active brain. *Pamela* included a multitude of details not essential to the story, but all bearing on it and increasing the richness of its total effect.[6] The

---

[3] *The History of the Works of the Learned* (2 vols., 1740), II, 439. (Issue for December, 1740). It is significant that a notice of *Pamela* in a journal of this caliber could be secured.

[4] Probably the first important notice of Richardson's epistolary technique was taken by the French critic Desfontaines in the *Bibliothèque britannique*, XXIX (1742), 70–71, 193–214.

[5] *Spectator* No. 375 (May 10, 1712).

[6] This elaboration of detail did not go down with all readers. The author of *The Life of Pamela* (1741) said (p. 185) that a gentleman had expressed his wonder that

uncompromising particularity of Richardson's mind led him to do something new with old materials. The novelty of *Pamela* lay not in the technical materials Richardson used, but in the extent to which he developed them.

"the Author had not told the exact Number of Pins *Pamela* had about her when she set out for Lincolnshire, and how many Rows of those Pins she bought for a Penny." Feminine readers, however, would have been likely to enjoy just such domestic details. See Ian Watt, *The Rise of the Novel* (London, 1957), p. 153.

William Park: From Fielding *and* Richardson

. . . modern critics such as Leslie Fiedler have been quick to point out that mid-eighteenth-century novels, particularly Richardson's, abound in . . . anti-aristocractic, middle-class sentiments, and that in many ways the books can be regarded as harbingers of forthcoming political revolutions.[1] What these critics too often forget to mention, however, is that both Richardson and Fielding have cast their middle-class notions into a nostalgic form. The novelists look back to what to them seemed to be the good old days of Queen Anne when the landed gentry had some wealth, power, and authority and could lead their private lives in an idyllic countryside, unaffected by party politics and factions.

From an eighteenth-century point of view, the happy man of the novel, living in his good society, must have seemed some kind of universal ideal. Just as the painter, according to Reynolds, discovers beauty at a mean between the extreme variety found in nature,[2] so the novelist finds virtue at this middle station between, on the one side, the nobility and aristocracy, and on the other, the artisans and laborers. Though goodness may be found in all spheres of life, the implication seems to be that the country gentleman always has been the best English type, the one who can best preserve the green world of the English countryside.

This static notion of happiness in the novels is accompanied by similar attitudes toward society and history. . . . Although novels about apprentices, bastards, and parish girls no doubt satisfied a yearn-

Reprinted by permission of the Modern Language Association from "Fielding and Richardson" by William Park, PMLA, LXXXI (October, 1966), 386–88. Copyright © 1966 by the Modern Language Association of America.

[1] *Love and Death in the American Novel* (New York, 1960). On p. 40, Fiedler says that the refusal to be raped was a metaphor of class war.

[2] Sir Joshua Reynolds, *The Idler*, No. 82 (10 Nov. 1759), *The Works of Samuel Johnson LL.D.* (London, 1816), VII, 329–334.

ing toward social mobility, the manner in which authors disguised the
rise of their heroes demonstrated at least an overt allegiance to a
system of class whose barriers were as inviolable as virtue itself.

The major exception to this generality occurs in *Pamela*. Pamela,
unlike Marivaux's Marianne and other virtuous girls, really comes
from the lower classes. She really rises, and in the first volume of her
story, her virtue is rewarded by marriage and a position in the genteel
world. Richardson then devoted the remaining three volumes to
apologizing for the demon he had created and trying to justify Mr. B.'s
rash act. In the end, we, and all Mr. B.'s friends and relations, realize
that Pamela is a freak. She is a prodigy. She is more genteel than
gentility itself. She becomes the model for the fashionable world. The
rich and titled send their daughters to learn at her feet. She advises
the clergy; she corrects Locke; and always she keeps her parents far
away on a farm in another country, fearful lest her other relatives
try to "move in." Richardson, sympathetic to Pamela and the prudent,
industrious, and rising class she represents, insists upon order and
tradition and denies the implications of his own creation. Pamela's
rise cannot, must not, be repeated.

His awareness of this conflict produced a great scene, one of the
best monuments in eighteenth-century fiction.[3] The B. family has
gone on an outing, leaving Pamela, who is slightly indisposed because
of her pregnancy, at home to write in her closet. She overhears voices,
laughter, verbal repulses which but encourage greater liberties, and
she looks through the keyhole and sees Polly Barlow and Mr. H., Lady
Davers' nephew. Obviously they had arranged a rendezvous in Pamela's
apartment, and the girl is about to give in and be ruined on Pamela's
own bed, when Pamela coughs, surprises the guilty pair, and puts a
stop to their amour. Right before her eyes she has seen a re-enactment
in a nightmarish manner of her own situation—the waiting maid
pursued by the gentleman. But all the values have shifted. The girl
is willing; the gentleman is a fop who cannot even write English; and
the genteel lady this time successfully breaks up the wicked and
socially upsetting liaison. For Pamela has become the lady; she is now
the agent of Lady Davers, aware that she acts for the Lady and aware
of the parallel between herself and Polly Barlow, a parallel which
makes it all the more important that she conduct herself with prudence, lest the world think that she and Mr. B. have set a bad example.
Only where waiting maids are Pamelas can they marry their masters,
and there is but one Pamela.

[3] *Pamela* (Oxford, 1929), III, 367–371.

Epilogue by *Bernard Kreissman:* From *Pamela–Shamela*

Some twelve years ago—to be precise, on December 12, 1948—J. Donald Adams, writing in the *New York Times Book Review*, remarked that Richardson's works were dead for the general reader. In view of the headline news of the day—the election of Truman, the impending war in Korea, the indictment of Alger Hiss—one would suppose that an obituary notice, even a premature one, might easily be overlooked. But the outcry of dissent evoked by this "rash statement" forced a hurried retraction from Adams.[1]

Unbeknownst to Adams and his readers, at this very time Pamela Andrews was alive and walking the soil of California. By a most remarkable stroke of fortune it came to the knowledge of one of the twentieth century's more prolific popular novelists, Mr. Upton Sinclair, that Pamela "had experienced a reincarnation." He promptly "sought her out and obtained permission to edit and publish the letters which she had written to her family over a period of several years."[2] The letters, published as *Another Pamela; or, Virtue Still Rewarded* (1950), are an account of her life from her sixteenth year up to her marriage two years later.

While there are differences in the two stories, in its essential elements Sinclair's redaction is *Pamela* in modern dress, with some superstructure added to the basic plot for the sake of twentieth-century plausibility. . . .

. . . Pamela Two drives as sharp a bargain as Pamela One, and has the forthrightness to say straight out that she *is* bargaining (p. 294); but she does not do so to gain material advantages and higher social status—instead, reversing the original Pamela, she is bargaining *away* from them. It is highly unlikely that *Another Shamela* could be written to expose *Another Pamela*, for there are simply no hidden motives to uncover.

When all this has been said, it ought to follow that Sinclair's heroine holds our affection more than does Richardson's, yet nothing could be farther from the truth. Richardson's Pamela is alive within

---

From *"Reincarnation" in* Pamela–Shamela, *by Bernard Kreissman (Lincoln, Neb.: University of Nebraska Press, 1960), pp. 75, 79–80. Copyright © 1960 by the University of Nebraska Press. Reprinted by permission of the publisher.*

[2] Upton Sinclair, *Another Pamela; or, Virtue Still Rewarded* (New York: Viking
[1] J. Donald Adams, "Speaking of Books," *The New York Times Book Review,* December 12, 1948, p. 2; December 26, 1948, p. 2; and January 9, 1949, p. 2.
Press, 1950), p. vii.

her scheming narrow world; she engages our attention, our delight, even our awe. Beside her, Sinclair's Pamela is a shadow, a wooden understudy essaying a star's role. We come now to a full realization of the effect of Richardson's style. Sinclair paid deference to Richardson's artistry even as he made wholesale changes in the ideological content of Pamela. While he seems to agree with the previous criticisms of B. and Williams as characters and the criticism of Richardson's prolixity, in his Pamela we find most of Richardson's stylistic mannerisms—the first person present indicative, the entreaties to Heaven, the little sentimental touches, the moralizing, the flood of trivia. But without the prima donna to carry them off the speeches fall flat. The mannerisms can be imitated, but it takes the spark of life to animate them. . . .

. . . In the original novel, Pamela occupies stage center throughout and is Richardson's voice for his ideas on all of eighteenth-century English life. Sinclair, by limiting the nature and extent of his Pamela's correspondence, limits her development as a character and is forced to introduce a number of extraneous social and political events to portray the twentieth-century world. Not only is the spotlight frequently off his leading lady, but at times she is lost from sight altogether behind a host of maudlin but distracting bit players.

What Sinclair's novel demonstrates above all is that a sounder philosophical point of view does not by any means insure a sounder work of art. Even with all the revisions suggested by the significant criticisms of Pamela incorporated into the new version, even with all her personal defects replaced by virtues, the result is not a better novel. *Pamela* is great because it is precisely what it is. Today no less than two hundred years ago it stands as a magnificent "picture of an atrocious prude," of "mock-modesty display'd," of "all the matchless arts of that young politician"—so great indeed that for another two hundred years we can expect Pamela to interest readers in her virtue, and critics in her virtuosity. The array of parody, burlesque, criticism, imitation, plagiarism, objection, and condemnation, from *Shamela* to *Another Pamela*, is a striking affirmation of the unquenchable vitality of the one and only, the incomparable, the original Pamela.

Chronology of Important Dates

	Richardson	Historical and Cultural Events
1688		Glorious Revolution; birth of Pope.
1689	Born in Derbyshire.	William and Mary.
1701	Merchant Taylors' School (?)	Queen Anne.
1704		Newton's *Opticks;* Battle of Blenheim.
1706	Apprenticed to John Wilde.	
1709		*The Tatler.*
1713		Treaty of Utrecht.
1714		George I; Pope's *Rape of the Lock.*
1715	Freeman of the Stationers' Co.	
1719	Established in business.	Defoe's *Robinson Crusoe.*
1721	Marries Martha Wilde.	Robert Walpole, Prime Minister; Montesquieu's *Persian Letters.*
1722	Takes over prosperous Leake business.	
1726		Swift's *Gulliver's Travels.*
1727		George II.
1732	Marries Elizabeth Leake.	
1733	*Apprentice's Vade Mecum.*	
1735		Hogarth's "Rake's Progress"
1739		Hume's *Treatise on Human Nature.*
1740	(Nov. 6) *Pamela,* Vols. I, II.	
1741	(Dec. 7) *Pamela,* Vols. III, IV.	(April) Fielding's *Shamela.*
1742		(Feb.) Fielding's *Joseph Andrews.*
1747	(Dec. 1) *Clarissa,* Vols. I, II.	
1748	(Apr. 28) *Clarissa,* Vols. III, IV. (Dec. 6) *Clarissa,* Vols. V–VII.	
1749		Fielding's *Tom Jones.*
1751		Diderot's *Encyclopédie.*

1753   (Nov. 13) *Grandison,* Vols. I–IV.
       (Dec. 11) *Grandison,* Vols. V, VI.
1754   (Mar. 14) *Grandison,* Vol. VII;
      Master of the Stationers' Co.

1755   Johnson's *Dictionary.*
1758   Voltaire's *Candide.*
1760   George III.
1761   (July 4) Dies.   Rousseau's *La Nouvelle Héloïse.*

Notes on the Editor and Contributors

ROSEMARY COWLER, editor of this volume, is Professor of English at Lake Forest College. She has contributed "Shadow and Substance: A Discussion of Pope's Correspondence" to *The Familiar Letter in the Eighteenth Century* (1966), and, with Maynard Mack, is preparing an edition of Pope's prose works.

R. F. BRISSENDEN is Senior Research Fellow in the History of Ideas at the Australian National University. His publications on eighteenth-century fiction include an edition for the Augustan Reprint Society of the *Prefaces, Hints of Prefaces and Postscript* to *Clarissa* (1964).

JOHN SAMUEL BULLEN is Associate Professor of English at Sonoma State College and Bibliographical Editor of *Western American Literature*.

DAVID DAICHES is Professor of English and Dean of the School of English and American Studies at the University of Sussex, England, after having taught previously at Cambridge, Cornell, and Edinburgh. Among his many critical works are *A Critical History of English Literature* (1960) and *The Novel and the Modern World* (1939, rev. ed. 1960).

ROBERT ADAMS DAY is Associate Professor of English at Queens College, City University of New York. In addition to *Told in Letters* (1966) he has written critical and bibliographical articles on early English fiction and on twentieth-century fiction and poetry—T. S. Eliot and Hart Crane.

LESLIE A. FIEDLER is currently visiting Professor of American Studies at the University of Sussex in England; among his many publications is his most recent *The Return of the Vanishing American*.

MORRIS GOLDEN, Associate Professor of English at the University of Massachusetts, is the author of *Richardson's Characters* (1963) and, most recently, *Fielding's Moral Psychology* (1966).

KATHERINE HORNBEAK is Professor Emerita of Smith College, where for thirty-two years she taught English, especially Augustan satire and seminars in Swift as well as Johnson and Boswell. In retirement she is working on some of the unpublished correspondence of Mrs. Elizabeth Montagu.

OWEN JENKINS is Professor of English at Carleton College.

A. M. KEARNEY is a lecturer at Chorley College of Education, England, and has published various articles on Richardson. At the moment he is doing research in nineteenth-century education.

M. KINKEAD–WEEKES, Senior Lecturer in English at the University of Kent at Canterbury, has published articles on Richardson, Kipling, Golding, and

Lawrence; edited an annotated selection of Pope; and, with Ian Gregor, written *William Golding, A Critical Study.* He is currently preparing a book on Richardson as well as the Richardson volume in the "Critical Heritage" series.

BERNARD KREISSMAN, at present Professor and Chief Librarian of the City College of the City University of New York, has edited Sir Walter Scott's *Life of John Dryden* and contributed to professional library journals.

ALBERT M. LYLES teaches at the University of Tennessee, where he is Assistant Professor of English. He is the author of *Methodism Mocked* and articles on Johnson and Gray.

CAREY MCINTOSH is Assistant professor of English at Harvard University, though he is currently on leave, engaged in writing a book on Samuel Johnson.

ALAN D. MCKILLOP has taught at Rice University since 1920 and, as he comments, "has paid particular attention to the eighteenth-century novelists." Two of the best-known products of that attention are *Samuel Richardson: Printer and Novelist* (1936) and *The Early Masters of English Fiction* (1956).

WILLIAM PARK teaches eighteenth-century literature at Sarah Lawrence College.

B. L. REID, Professor of English at Mount Holyoke College, has published short stories and poems, critical essays particularly on eighteenth century and modern writers, and books on Gertrude Stein and William Butler Yeats, with a biography, *The Man from New York: John Quinn and his Friends,* to be published shortly.

SHELDON SACKS, Professor of English and Linguistics at the University of Chicago, has taught at the University of Texas, at the University of California at Berkeley, and, as Visiting Professor, at the University of Rome. In addition to *Fiction and the Shape of Belief* (1964), he has edited, with Ralph Rader, *An Analytic Reader* (1964).

GEORGE SHERBURN was, at the time of his death in 1962, Professor Emeritus of English, Harvard University. One of the most distinguished scholars of the eighteenth century, he was particularly renowned for his work on Pope, though one of his very last endeavors was an abridgement of *Clarissa.*

IAN WATT, Professor of English at Stanford University, formerly taught at St. John's College, Cambridge; the University of California at Berkeley; and the University of East Anglia at Norwich. He is the author of *The Rise of the Novel: Studies in Defoe, Richardson and Fielding* (1957) and of numerous essays on eighteenth- and twentieth-century subjects.

Selected Bibliography

Although the essays included in this volume themselves constitute a good working bibliography, the reader should bear in mind that the selections taken from longer works can only partially represent the originals, which should be consulted for further material. Particularly helpful as complete studies, for example, are Ian Watt's *The Rise of the Novel*, R. F. Brissenden's concise volume *Samuel Richardson* (in the Writers and Their Work series), and Morris Golden's *Richardson's Characters;* and though Leslie A. Fiedler's *Love and Death in the American Novel* is concerned with Richardson, Fielding, and the Gothic Novel in their influence on the history of the American novel, his treatment of Richardson is perceptive as well as provocative.

In addition, any student of *Pamela*, or of Richardson generally, will be indebted to the scholarship of Alan D. McKillop and of William M. Sale, Jr. The former's *Samuel Richardson: Printer and Novelist* (Chapel Hill, 1936) and *The Early Masters of English Fiction* (Lawrence, Kansas, 1956) are classic studies, critical and historical surveys of Richardson's literary career. The latter's *Samuel Richardson: Master Printer* (Ithaca, New York, 1950) complements these with an extensive investigation of Richardson's activity as printer—background necessary for a complete understanding of his life and writings. Mr. Sale's bibliographic study, *Samuel Richardson: A Bibliographic Record of his Literary Career with Historical Notes* (New Haven, 1936), also should be cited, as well as Francesco Cordasco's *Samuel Richardson: A List of Critical Studies Published from 1896 to 1946* (Brooklyn, 1948). Of historical interest are two volumes in the Augustan Reprint series; No. 21, "Critical Remarks on *Sir Charles Grandison, Clarissa,* and *Pamela*," edited by Mr. McKillop; and No. 48, Richardson's own "Introduction to *Pamela*," edited by S. W. Baker. And recent and valuable is John Carroll's edition of the correspondence, *Selected Letters of Samuel Richardson* (Oxford, 1964), a collection of "those letters or passages from the letters that bear on the themes and characters of Richardson's novels, on his craftsmanship and literary judgments, and on his own personality."

TWENTIETH CENTURY
INTERPRETATIONS

MAYNARD MACK, *Series Editor*
Yale University

NOW AVAILABLE
Collections of Critical Essays
ON

ADVENTURES OF HUCKLEBERRY FINN
ALL FOR LOVE
ARROWSMITH
AS YOU LIKE IT
BLEAK HOUSE
THE BOOK OF JOB
DUBLINERS
THE DUCHESS OF MALFI
EURIPIDES' ALCESTIS
THE FROGS
SIR GAWAIN AND THE GREEN KNIGHT
GRAY'S ELEGY
THE GREAT GATSBY
GULLIVER'S TRAVELS
HAMLET
HENRY IV, PART TWO
HENRY V
THE ICEMAN COMETH
JULIUS CAESAR
KEATS'S ODES
OEDIPUS REX
THE OLD MAN AND THE SEA
PAMELA
THE PORTRAIT OF A LADY

A Portrait of the Artist as a Young Man
Samson Agonistes
The Scarlet Letter
The Sound and the Fury
Tom Jones
Twelfth Night
Utopia
Walden
The Waste Land
Wuthering Heights